W9-DGI-083

The Science of Smell

Approximate scale models of three insect-attracting chemical molecules.
Left: The natural attractant that draws the drone to the queen bee.
Top: The synthetic melon fly attractant, 'Cue-Lure.'
Bottom: 'Gyplure', the synthetic analogue of the natural
  gypsy moth attractant.

THE SCIENCE

OF SMELL

R. H. Wright

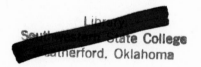
Library
Southwestern State College
Weatherford. Oklahoma

BASIC BOOKS, INC., PUBLISHERS

New York

©George Allen & Unwin Ltd, 1964
Library of Congress Catalog Card Number: 64-20274
Printed in the United States of America

In Science, it is when we take some interest in the great discoverers and their lives that it becomes endurable, and only when we begin to trace the development of ideas that it becomes fascinating.

JAMES CLERK MAXWELL

178857

This is a survey of olfaction and olfactory responses: to be comprehended by intelligent laymen and scientific specialists, both. It touches on fish migration, infrared spectroscopy, nerve physiology, organic chemistry, psychophysics, communication theory, animal behaviour, and quantum mechanics.

Not many scientists are familiar with all these, so that one who writes for them all must use a language they all know, and there are two choices. The first is to use the precise and exact technical language of each specialty and let the reader make what he can of sentences like this: 'The parts of the brain involved in the transmission of olfactory signals are the olfactory bulb, tract, and parts of the basal areas of the forebrain including the prepiriform and paraamygdaloid complex, and parts of the corpus striatum'.

The alternative is to use ordinary English as far as it can be pushed, on the principle that it is the common language of educated laymen and of scientists outside their own specialty. This is what I have tried to do, but the boundary between educated English and technical jargon is neither sharp nor constant. I must ask the specialists who find my treatment of unfamiliar fields useful, to bear with me when I come to their own; and I hope that the non-scientists will find this book like the curate's egg: 'Quite good in parts'.

R.H.W.
Vancouver
May, 1963

CONTENTS

ILLUSTRATIONS

ILLUSTRATIONS

1

How Scientists Work

THIS book is about two things.

I will try to tell something of the fascination and the importance of the so-far unsolved mystery of smell, because it is a problem that has held my interest for a long time and because I think it is one of the most neglected fields of scientific enquiry.

I will also try to show something of the machinery of scientific investigation as it functions not just at the laboratory bench but also in the technical literature and in the minds of the working scientists —which are as much a part of the apparatus of science as the glassware and electronic equipment of a laboratory.

The nature of this thing called Science is so important, and to many people so unknown or mis-known, that my second objective may be the most valuable in the end. If my book is no more than an account of the state of our knowledge of smells and smelling up to 5 p.m. on a certain afternoon, it will soon lose its point; but if it is also a portrait of science at work, then its inevitable technical obsolescence will not matter so much.

The field of smells and smelling is one in which I have worked myself, and therefore the subject matter and manner of presentation will naturally be biased. This is a fact of life, but the machinery of science-at-work is arranged to take care of my bias as impartially and impersonally as it takes care of any other man's bias, and the fact that this is done so surely and so systematically is one of the things that gives organized science its enormous power to change the world.

It is customary in formal scientific writing to speak of one's self in the third person, like this: 'In a previous communication (Wright, 1956) the writer showed that . . .' and so on. This is good when attention is to be focused on the work rather than the worker, but I will not follow the practice here, partly because it sounds a little stilted, and partly because it will be much clearer that scientific research is an intensely personal activity if I now and then call myself 'I' than if I retreat into the faceless anonymity of the third person.

Science is inescapably collective. Its essential interdependence

1

follows from the fact that it does not concern itself with the whole of human experience but only that part of it which is perceptible to more than one observer. There are great ranges of personal, mainly emotional, experience which lie outside the scope of science because they cannot be reproduced and independently verified. When the collectiveness of science is overlooked (as it so often is) a queer sort of blind spot results, as, for example, when a highly regarded mathematician concluded an article on mathematics with the words:

'Curiously enough, I do not remember ever having seen a sustained argument by any author which, starting from philosophical or theological premises likely to meet with general acceptance, reached the conclusion that a praiseworthy ordering of one's life is to devote it to mathematics.'

But if science is a collective enterprise it is an enterprise in which individuals take part. Therefore we must consider everything from two points of view.

Take, first, the objectives of science. There are the collective objectives of Science-as-a-Going-Concern and there are the personal objectives of each individual scientist, and they are not by any means the same. The personal motives are as diverse as the scientists themselves, but they usually include varying proportions of intellectual curiosity and a desire for recognition, both reinforced by the real attraction of work that offers a unique combination of intellectual and manual effort. In contrast with these varied personal objectives, the collective objective of science—the thing that makes Society-as-a-Whole support Science-as-a-Whole, is quite simple: it pays.

The same dualism is apparent also in the scientific method. The scientific method has been defined in many ways, most of them rather unsatisfactory. One reads of such matters as concomitant variation and the inductive-deductive method, which come nowhere near to giving the general reader an appreciation of the real stuff of science, to say nothing of its spirit. This is because they do not separate the individual and the collective aspects, which is unfortunate because both personally and collectively science is one of the most exciting adventures the individual or the race has ever undertaken.

There have been many attempts to glamourize science as a personal adventure, but I do not think it is anywhere exhibited better than by a single word in the manuscript scientific diary kept by Michael Faraday. Faraday was one of the two or three most original and creative scientists of the last century, and on any reckoning his was one of the ten most powerful scientific minds the world has so far seen. He believed in the unity of Nature—that it should be possible

2

to bring all the phenomena of nature into a single system of thought —and he made it his life's work to provide an experimental base for his opinion. On September 13, 1845, he wrote the following account of an experiment to find out whether magnetism and optics are connected:

'September 13, 1845. A piece of heavy glass which was 2 inches by 1.8 inches by 0.5 of an inch thick, being silicoborate of lead and polished on the two shortest edges was experimented with. It gave no effect when the same magnetic poles or the contrary poles were on opposite sides (as respects the course of the polarized ray) nor where the same poles were on the same side either with the constant or intermitting current. . . .'

And now, after all these negative results we suddenly have a little word of three letters, not written, but printed in enormous capitals and underlined three times: 'BUT'.

'. . . BUT when the contrary magnetic poles were on the same side, there was an effect produced on the polarized ray, and thus the magnetic force and light were proved to have relation to each other. This fact will most likely prove exceedingly fertile . . .' and so on.

No one seeing that great printed and underlined BUT in the middle of the page can suppose that Faraday was the detached, cold-minded observer that the textbooks usually present (quite wrongly) as the ideal scientist.

Personally, each scientist sooner or later finds his own private formula. Faraday, for example, built his life's work on a general principle. He said:

'I have long held an opinion, almost amounting to conviction, that the various forms under which the forces of matter are made manifest have one common origin, or, in other words, are so directly related and mutually dependent that they are converted as it were one into another, and possess equivalents of power in their action.'

He made it his business to seek out and discover objective evidence for these inter-relations. At the same time, he was clear-sighted enough to see the collective side of what he was about, for he said:

'I have rather been desirous of discovering new facts and relations . . . than in exalting the force of those already obtained, being assured that the latter would find their full development hereafter.'

Kekulé, whose invention of structural formulae made modern organic chemistry possible, had another prescription. 'Let us learn to dream' he said:

3

'Let us learn to dream and then perhaps we shall find out the truth. But let us beware of publishing our dreams until they have been put to the proof by the waking understanding.'

The story of his dreams about carbon chains and the benzene ring, and what came of them, are known to every scientist.

Einstein had yet another formula:

'The supreme task of the physicist,' he said, 'is to arrive at those universal elementary laws from which the cosmos can be built up by pure deduction. There is no logical path to these laws; only intuition resting on sympathetic understanding of experience, can reach them.'

The common thread that runs through all these highly personal patterns seems to be imaginative thought about the results of experiment.

2

How Science Works

IF on its personal side the scientific method is rather elastic, on its collective side it is much more rigid and formal. It consists of an apparatus by which knowledge can be organized in a very fruitful way, and it is worth while to consider it in some detail.

At the bottom we have data, which comprise the recorded observations of verifiable phenomena. A phenomenon is some object or event—or combination of them—which we perceive with our senses and which is intrinsically capable of being perceived by more than one person. The sense organs are machines of the same type in normal human beings and so they carry approximately the same sense impressions to the brain. This makes the Universe basically similar for all normal people, and science concerns itself only with those aspects of it which *are* similar in this sense.

When a phenomenon is carefully examined and the observations are recorded, the records are called data. Data may be obtained by what we call 'bare observations' where the observer has no control over the influences acting on the phenomenon, or by 'experimental observations' ('experiments' for short) where he does control at least some of these influences. History shows that progress is usually much faster when we can use experiments to replace bare observations. When we can't, theory often provides a way around the difficulty as we shall see presently.

An observation of either kind must be made as carefully and impartially as circumstances permit, and because science is collective it must be recorded and communicated to others in writing. Accurate description and communication require a clear understanding of the meaning of each word used, for thoughts must eventually be cast into words. As we become aware of more phenomena in more detail we need new words to record our observations. This explains the need for a precise scientific terminology or 'jargon'. (But it can be overdone. My own pet hate is 'hypothesize' which never means anything more than 'assume' and is used only for show. 'Hypothecate' which is sometimes used in the same way, shows ignorance as well.)

Care and impartiality in the gathering and recording of data and the independent checking of data by different observers, are the corner-stone of science. The way to be sure is to be unsure. Darwin is reported to have said that Nature will tell you a direct lie if she can!

Sometimes it is said that science deals with facts. Whether this is correct depends on the meaning attached to the word 'fact'. To most people, 'Fact' implies 'Truth'. It needs very little experience in making experiments or constructing sentences to know that every measurement has a residuum of error and every sentence is only an approximation to the thought of the writer. It is therefore better to say that science deals with data—that is, with recorded observations—and that the data are almost certainly not true but are the best available approximation to it. Ultimate truth can only be hinted at.

When data have been collected, sorted, arranged, classified, re-checked, looked-at, and thought about, then certain regularities may appear. That is, it may be possible to correlate one set of observations with another or the appearance of one kind of behaviour with the incidence of one set of influences. Such a correlation can then be formulated into a generalization or 'Law of Nature'. This is merely a statement that under certain circumstances certain phenomena can generally or always be observed. Many laws are statistical, in that they apply accurately to large assemblages of atoms or animals but are no more than statements of probability when applied to individuals or small groups. A law correlates observables; it does not correlate cause-and-effect. 'People who own Rolls-Royce automobiles do not die of tuberculosis' may be a perfectly good generalization but it has nothing to do with either the cause of TB or the effect of owning an expensive motor car.

The purpose of a generalization is to enable observations to be transferred from one case to another. The transfer is naturally attended by some uncertainty at first, and it is an essential part of the scientific method to subject every generalization to the widest possible test of experiment and observation. It is by some people considered a crime to 'generalize beyond one's data'. In fact it is a crime not to, because this is the quickest way to establish the limits within which a generalization holds. Few laws are always and universally exact and it is as important to know where they do not hold as where they do.

While it is true that generalizations are formulated on the basis of data, very often a generalization may be suspected by the observer before he has any data to support it. This is perfectly legitimate and the observer is no less competent or scientific so long as his preconceptions do not affect the integrity of his data. A preconception used as a guide in making observations or experiments is called a 'working hypothesis'. Later chapters will show that working hypotheses are

6

among the most useful tools of science when properly used. 'Scientific intuition' is essentially a highly developed ability to generate working hypotheses.

When we have established a number of generalizations, the next step is to tie them together by means of a theory. To do this, we make certain assumptions and with their help we show that one set of generalizations is logically deducible from another apparently unconnected set of generalizations.

For example, on the basis of certain observations we have a set of generalizations, known as the Laws of Motion, which describe the behaviour of moving bodies; and we have another and differently derived set of generalizations which describe the behaviour of gases and are called the Gas Laws. By making certain assumptions to the effect that gases are composed of small, freely moving, elastic particles, we are able to show that the Gas Laws are a logical consequence of the Laws of Motion (always given the assumption about the structure). This amounts to a tremendous consolidation of knowledge since it brings the motions of the heavenly bodies and the properties of gases into a single conceptual scheme which includes many other kinds of motion as well. This is an important accomplishment but it is only one outcome of the theory.

If we examine the further consequences of our reasoning, we are able to predict new generalizations, such as a relation between the density of a gas and the rate with which it will escape through a small hole.

If these predictions turn out to be correct, then evidently the theory has acted as a catalyst to the acquisition of new knowledge by showing us where to look for new generalizations. Thus the accumulation of data becomes less of a magpie collection of facts and more of a systematized hunt for needed information. It is the existence of classification and generalization, and above all of theory that makes science an *organized* body of knowledge.

We are now in a position to frame clear definitions of the words 'theory' and 'hypothesis' and to draw a simple distinction between them. A hypothesis is a more or less plausible assumption used in constructing a theory. (This is, of course, different from the 'working hypothesis' already defined.) A theory is a process by which a whole body of knowledge, data, generalizations, and assumptions, is knit together by a process of logical reasoning. Most textbooks do not draw a clear distinction between the words theory and hypothesis and leave a vague and unsatisfactory feeling that a hypothesis is an ill-found theory and a theory is a hypothesis not quite so ill-found.

It is essential that the number of assumptions used in constructing

7

a theory should be kept at a minimum. This principle is sometimes called 'Occam's Razor' from the name of the medieval philosopher who propounded it. New theories replace old ones because new generalizations have to be fitted in or because someone has found a way to reduce the number of assumptions that have to be made.

Evidently logic is an integral part of all theories. Logic consists of a set of agreed rules which normal and civilized men have agreed to use in reasoning from premises to conclusions. There are two sorts of logic: qualitative or common logic and quantitative or mathematical logic. When our data and generalizations are quantitative we need mathematics to work out a theory that will show the quantitative relations between them and predict new quantitative generalizations. This is why so much scientific theory is mathematical.

Besides linking generalizations that are already known and predicting new ones, theories serve a third purpose: they often enable us to bridge the gap between a field where experiments are possible and one where we can make only bare observations. This can be very valuable in fields like astrophysics and human and animal genetics.

The scientific way of organizing knowledge is a fairly recent invention, historically speaking, and it is the means by which science has grown so rapidly and shown such astounding success in solving practical problems. Its main social impact is a destruction or alteration of the material bases of old-established customs and institutions. This is something that has happened before, but the thing that makes the present situation unique is the rapidity of the advance, that is, the violence of the impact. It seems likely that people with a scientific turn of mind have existed in all ages. The growth of science in the past two or three centuries has not been due to a series of unique biological accidents producing men like Newton or Darwin, but rather to a social system that gives men an opportunity to exercise their talents and a system of organization and communication that enables them to do it collectively.

It has been said that by ignoring everything that is not collectively observable, science is ignoring the most important parts of human experience, and so can never be on the same elevated plane as the 'Humanities'.

I think this is all wrong.

Suppose that you, being what you are and knowing what you know, were to find yourself set down in an isolated village with an epidemic of typhoid fever going on. There are three, and only three, things you can do:

1. You can run away;
2. You can nurse and comfort the sick;

8

3. You can try to clean up the water supply.

Assuming that you do not run away, is it any less humanitarian to try to stop the epidemic and prevent future suffering by working on the water supply (even if it means neglecting the present sufferers) than to ignore the future and try to relieve the present suffering? I do not think (2) is any more (or any less) humanitarian than (3). One kind of person will do one thing—and that will be right for him—and another will do the other—equally rightly. What *is* a waste of time is for the two kinds of Samaritans to abuse each other as inhuman materialists or ineffectual sentimentalists. This is what usually happens, so that the people who run away get off scot-free!*

* Even the run-aways serve a useful purpose for they ensure that the species will be continued should our imaginary epidemic completely wipe out our hypothetical village.

3

A Problem

HAVING seen how science in general is organized and carried on, let us now watch it in action in a particular case.

One of the most remarkable things about smell is that it is a non-directional sense that can produce a directed response. A creature with two ears can locate the direction of a sound with considerable precision, and even with only one ear the direction from which the sound is loudest can be estimated approximately. Hearing is directional and so is sight, but smelling is not and neither is taste. A meal tastes the same whether the kitchen lies to the right or left of the diner, because we taste or smell things when their molecules make physical contact with sensory organs that can only tell us that the molecules have arrived but not the direction they came from.

The problem of tracking a scent to its source is fairly easy for a land animal such as a dog. It can run to and fro with its nose to the ground, picking out the trail it has been set to follow and disregarding all the other smells along the way. If it loses the scent it can begin to circle and search because it remembers the right scent even though it no longer smells it. When it regains the scent it goes forward rather than back over its own track because all the time other parts of its mind have been registering and remembering where it has been already. The next day it can track down a different odour and the day after that yet another, because it is not limited to the perception of just one scent.

The problem is different and a little simpler when an animal such as a deer scents a hunter who has been incautious enough to approach from up wind. The scent rings an alarm in the animal's brain, whereupon it lifts its head, sniffs the air, and turns this way and that until it feels the wind full in its face. This tells it the direction of the danger and it makes off another way.

For the dog to track its quarry across a field, or for the deer to avoid the hunter successfully, a complicated sensory apparatus must feed a large amount of information into a rather highly developed brain. This amount of brain work is absolutely out of the question for an insect for the simple reason that its brain is thousands of times too small.

10

In its very limited all-up weight, a mosquito or a fruit fly has to provide for many things: fuel, power plant, landing gear, and (what no aeroplane has to carry) the complete plans and specifications and the basic machinery for making a new fly. Therefore its sensory apparatus and brain capacity must be kept to a minimum. Notwithstanding this, many quite small insects can track an attractive scent to its source and do it surprisingly quickly, and what is more curious still, they do it through the trackless air where there are no landmarks and where the scent itself moves with every rustle of the leaves. Experiments have been reported in which a female moth no bigger than a postage stamp has been hidden in a paper box and found by marked males released a long way down wind. In at least one case the insects had to fly several miles over open water to reach a small island where some females had been placed.

This is a wonderful achievement which becomes more so the more we examine it.

Let us first get rid of an elementary misapprehension, which is that a flying insect can respond like a deer by turning so as to feel the wind full in its face. The deer can do this because it has its feet on the ground and can fix itself in one place while the wind blows past it. The same is true for an insect as long as it is not flying, but it ceases to be true the moment the insect leaves the ground. When a creature is air-borne (whether insect, bird, or man) it has nothing to brace itself against and so must drift with the wind like thistledown or a free balloon. If it has the means to move itself through the air, that is, if it has muscles and wings or an engine and propellor, it can create its own wind, but this will have the same force against its face no matter which direction it takes with respect to the real wind-over-the-ground. The case is similar to that of a ship far out in the ocean: it can not feel the ocean currents unless it has some fixed land-mark or sky-mark to steer by. If an insect or a bird or aviator can see the ground or the heavenly bodies, it can correct for drift, but not otherwise, and so it is an interesting problem to find out how an almost completely brainless insect can make its way so surely up wind to the source of an attractive scent.

The working out of this problem (as far as it has been worked out) makes quite a good case study of how scientific research is carried on. I will tell the story as nearly as possible in the way it happened because it is instructive to see, among other things, how rewarding a mistake can be.

As always in beginning a new investigation, the technical literature was searched to make sure the problem had not already been solved. This turned up several interesting facts. First was the undoubted correctness of the basic assumption that male insects are in many cases guided to the females by an attracting scent, and not by radio waves or some kind of extra-sensory perception. The actual chemical has been isolated and identified in several cases and can be used as a lure to catch the males in traps where there are no females but only minute traces of the female scent. Several writers have remarked that the male insects must have an amazingly powerful sense of smell because the purified sex-odour had only a slight odour to man, and in minute traces no odour at all. Of course, this is nonsense because there is no reason why the human nose and the insect nose should be sensitive to the same smells. What has a strong smell to us may have only a weak smell or no smell at all to an insect, and *vice versa*.

The important thing was to make sure that there would be enough molecules of the attractive scent down wind from a female to give the male some kind of signal. In order to check this, I looked up the technical literature on how war-time poison-gas clouds travel with the wind. Meteorologists, like Sir O. G. Sutton, have worked out the mathematical theory of how the strength or concentration of a gas cloud falls off as it moves down wind from a point source located at ground level. It is a very difficult problem to analyze exactly, and rather drastic assumptions have to be made about such things as the smoothness of the ground and the steadiness of the wind. The final result is a complicated but usable formula which has been verified reasonably well by actual measurements of gas clouds.

With this formula I could calculate how many molecules of attractive scent there would be on the average in each cubic milli-meter of air at various distances down wind from where a female was releasing them. The calculation showed, for example, that if the scent was given off at a steady rate of one microgram per second into a wind of one mile per hour, the average concentration of the odourous molecules a mile and a half straight down wind would be about 60 per cubic millimeter. This is a pretty small number, but the mathematical formula gives the average concentration and the actual odour cloud is filamentous with localized zones where the concentration is much higher than this with intervening zones where it is much lower. Moreover, the male insects that depend on scent to locate the females usually have rather large and highly developed antennae which sweep up the odourous molecules in a fairly large volume of air as the insect flies along. It is fair to suppose that the insect samples the air in this way for a short interval of time during which it collects odourous molecules and stores their impulses before releasing them in a single burst to its brain. In many (and perhaps all) animals there is a basic electrical rhythm in the central nervous system with a frequency of around 50 cycles per second which could provide the timing mechanism for such a collecting scheme. If we suppose that the male flies at a speed of 2 miles per hour through the air and that its antennae have a cross-sectional area of 2 square millimeters, then in one-fiftieth of a second its antennae could sweep up on the average about 2000 molecules of the scent. This should be quite enough to give rise to a smell sensation.

This calculation is necessarily very approximate and contains a great many arbitrary assumptions. The final numerical answer can quite easily be too high or too low by a factor of 3, but it is not likely to be out by a factor of more than 10. The uncertainty does not really matter because the object of the calculation was simply to make sure that even if the scent is released at as low a rate as one microgram per second, there will be a substantial number of scent molecules available for the male insect to pick up at a distance of more than a mile away. If there is more than one female then of course the situation is that much improved, and the fact that the male ends up by locating one particular female does not mean that he was homing in on her right from the start.

What this calculation showed was simply that the effectiveness of an insect sex-attractant scent is interesting and remarkable, but it is in no way miraculous. In a broader way it shows how research in one field (in this case meteorology and gas warfare) gave results that could be turned to good use in a very different connection. Therein lies the unity of science.

The calculation also disposed of another simple way the insect might be supposed to gain a directional clue from a nondirectional sense. It is easy to suppose that it has only to fly in the direction that makes the smell sensation grow stronger. There are several reasons why this will not work.

For one thing, as the scent moves down wind and gets more dilute by mixing with the air, the average intensity dies away so slowly that an insect that picked up the scent might have to fly a long way—perhaps a quarter of a mile—before the average smell strength changed noticeably. More than that, the average strength of the scent and its actual strength from instant to instant are not at all the same thing. Anyone who has watched the smoke drifting away from a cigarette will have seen that it does not form a nice fuzzy cloud, densest along the center line and getting steadily thinner towards the edges, which is the way the mathematical formula pictures it. On the contrary, the smoke moves down wind in a complex pattern of streamers or filaments that constantly twist and curl and break up into new filaments. It would be quite impossible for an

13

insect to back-track along one of these filaments, and if it flew up the axis of the plume its sensation would not be one of steadily increasing odour strength, but rather a bumpy succession of alternating strong and weak smells as it flew in and out of the filaments. The fact that its smelling organs are located externally on the antennae would make this irregularity in the sensation especially noticeable.

The question of how a flying insect can achieve a precisely directed result from an undirected smell has no obvious answers.

The check of the scientific literature showed that the difficulty of determining wind direction and so correcting for drift had been largely neglected by entomologists. There were several technical articles that merely remarked that an attractive scent would make an insect fly toward the source (which was necessarily up wind), but there was no consideration given to the question of how it could know which way that was. At least one experimenter did realize the difficulty and study it systematically. J. S. Kennedy put mosquitoes in a little wind tunnel which was arranged so that he could project a moving pattern of light and dark spots on the walls or floor below the insects as they flew along. In this way he could create an illusion of wind movement and see how the mosquitoes responded.

When an insect, or a man in an aeroplane, flies straight down wind, he will see objects on the ground appear dead ahead and pass directly under him and finally vanish behind him. If he flies straight up wind, and if the wind is not too strong, he will see objects move under him in the same general way, but they will seem to move more slowly because his speed over the ground is slowed by the head wind. Straight up wind and straight down wind produce a generally similar visual pattern except that the movement seems slower when moving up wind.

If the movement is not straight up or down wind but is diagonally across the wind, the objects on the ground will not appear to come from straight ahead and disappear straight out behind, but they will appear to move under the insect (or the aeroplane) at an angle to its long axis. Insects have compound eyes which should make them very sensitive to this kind of movement over objects below them. Finally, it should be remarked that if the wind is so strong that the insect can not make headway against it and is carried backward, then the apparent movement of objects on the ground will be reversed and they will appear from behind and disappear out in front. Most insects find this very disturbing and usually land as quickly as they can.

What Kennedy did with his mosquitoes was to combine an actual measured wind through his cage with spots that could be moved in such a way as to mislead the mosquitoes as to the direction of the wind, or its strength, or both. In this way he showed that the mosquitoes could fly systematically up wind only if they could see the ground below them, and that with a rather light wind of around a quarter of a mile per hour they had to fly rather close to the ground in order to be guided effectively. With stronger winds they could fly higher and still set an up-wind course, but there was a limit when the wind became too strong and they refused to fly at all.

These experiments were significant but they did not wholly answer my question of how a male moth can use a non-directional smell to direct its course to the exact place where the smell originates. Kennedy himself realized this, for he said in his articles, 'With regard to the question of host finding . . . it is maintained here that flying orientation to a wind-borne scent is not, in a direct sense, easily conceivable'. And again, 'There is no apparent means by which freely flying insects orient themselves directly to the warmth, moisture, or odour of an air current'. The best he could conclude was that the scent triggered off an up-wind flight that somehow continued until the goal was reached.

This was a substantial advance, however, because it did show that mosquitoes at any rate do depend on their eyes to correct for wind drift while in flight. It did not explain how an insect could do this at night or while flying over rather smooth water which could not provide much in the way of fixed landmarks by which the course could be set. More than that, it did not provide any mechanism by which the insect could regain the scent if it lost it by moving off to one side or by overshooting the target.

REFERENCES

M. BEROZA. 'Insect Attractants are Taking Hold', *Agricultural Chemicals*, 37–40, July, 1960.

V. G. DETHIER. *Chemical Insect Attractants and Repellents*. Blakiston Co., Philadelphia, 1947.

J. S. KENNEDY. 'The Visual Responses of Flying Mosquitoes', *Proc. Zool. Soc., Ser. A*, **109**, 221–242, 1939.

O. G. SUTTON. 'The Problem of Diffusion in the Lower Atmosphere', *Quart. J. Roy. Met. Soc.*, **73**, 257–280, 1947.

O. G. SUTTON. 'The Application to Micrometeorology of the Theory of Turbulent Flow Over Rough Surfaces', *Quart. J. Roy. Met. Soc.*, **75**, 335–350, 1949.

R. H. WRIGHT. 'The Olfactory Guidance of Flying Insects', *Canadian Entomologist*, **90**, 81–89, 1958.

4

An Answer

THAT was the position when I began thinking about the problem of insect guidance by scent. I was particularly impressed by the reports of insects flying at night or over open water and still succeeding in finding their mates. This seemed to show that some insects at least might be able to locate the source of a scent even if they had no fixed landmarks below them to steer by. After all, I argued, Kennedy's experiments were done with mosquitoes which might not work in the same way as moths or fruit flies. And so I began to wonder whether there might be some kind of structure in the odour cloud itself that could tell the insect which way to fly and so make visual contact with the ground unnecessary.

I spent a good many hours looking at smoke clouds in an improvized wind tunnel and taking photographs of them, and I even 'cut' slices out of the clouds by darkening the tunnel and lighting up the smoke with a ribbon of light from a narrow slit. The general result was to make me vividly aware of the very complex, filamentous structure of the real smoke or odour trail—so different from the averaged picture given by the mathematical formula—and emphasized the 'bumpiness' of any smell sensation the insect would get while flying through it. In the end I evolved a working hypothesis or tentative theory of how the flying insects could be guided by smell.

Because of the structure of the odour cloud, it seemed certain that the insect with its sensory apparatus mounted externally on the antennae would necessarily perceive the smell as a series of pulses at irregular intervals rather than as a continuous sensation. Moreover, as it moved in towards the centre of the cloud, and as it got nearer to the source, the pulses should come closer together; and if it moved out of the cloud or down wind away from the source they should get farther apart. Thus it seemed that there was a sort of direction-sign in the odour cloud that a flying insect might use, and the way it might use it could be something like this.

While it was in free flight and before it entered the cloud, the insect could search by flying a series of rather long zig-zags. If, when it entered the cloud, its tendency to turn was inhibited as long as the interval between pulses tended to get shorter, it would be led generally in the right direction, toward the source. If it started to move out of the cloud or away from the source, the interval between pulses would lengthen, and this lengthening could release the inhibition on the tendency to turn. If this caused the insect to abandon its fixed flight path and make a series of short, violent zig-zags, it would be likely to locate a path in which the pulse interval once more tended to get smaller. The following very simple series of signals and responses should therefore enable an insect to home on an odour source with considerable precision and without benefit of 'ground fixes':

Signal	*Response*
None	. Long zig-zags
Pulses at decreasing intervals	. No zig-zags
Pulses at increasing intervals	. Short zig-zags

This is a variant of a well-known guidance mechanism that is believed to be used by various kinds of lowly creatures and is called 'klinokinesis'. Wood lice, for example, need a rather moist environment or they dry out and die. As long as they are in that kind of environment they do not move about very much. If the surroundings get a little too dry they start to move around, and their movement is characterized by a tendency to change direction in a completely random way. It has been observed, however, that they turn more and more frequently when conditions are getting worse, that is dryer, and they turn less frequently if the humidity begins to increase. It is clear that this mechanism will turn the animal away from the direction in which conditions get more hostile, and make it press forward when conditions are getting better—and it is completely automatic. The name 'klinokinesis' is intended to express this control of the direction by a modification in the frequency of a completely random series of turns.

Generally speaking, if we superimpose even a small element of system or purpose on an otherwise random process, the end result is precisely calculable—a fact that is well known to casino operators who need only to fix a house percentage to be sure of making a satisfactory profit regardless of the wins or losses of the individual gamblers.

The theory of olfactory guidance I had provisionally arrived at was essentially one that put the random element in the insect: it assumed that the insect would turn in a random way and that the turning tendency would be increased or decreased by signals received from the environment. It was (and for that matter still is) a perfectly good theory, and better than some because it could be tested experimentally in the following way.

17

The first thing was to choose a suitable insect and to work out a way of observing it while letting it fly as nearly naturally as possible.

Ordinary fruit flies (*Drosophila melanogaster*) such as are found on bunches of bananas were chosen because they are easy to rear in captivity and have a well-developed ability to locate fermenting fruit. My associate, Mr. Kellogg, then built a large plywood wind tunnel 2 feet square and 12 feet long so that the insects could fly about quite freely and without feeling the confining effects of narrow passages and sharp turns. The tunnel had a glass top and bottom so that we could watch them as they tried to locate a bit of over-ripe banana at the up-wind end of the tunnel. We sometimes took moving pictures so as to slow down their movements, and we often ran the films backward so as to back-track the successful fruit-seekers in the hope of seeing how they did it. We could also project moving patches of light on the floor of the tunnel, as Kennedy did, to confuse them as to the wind direction.

It very soon turned out that so far as fruit flies are concerned they need to see the ground under them if they are to find an up-wind target. By moving the projected pattern of light spots in various ways we could make them fly with the wind when they thought they were flying against it, or we could make them fly at an angle to the true wind direction so that they sheared off to one side and went past the bait. We could even make the fictitious wind so strong that they refused to fly at all. (Fruit flies don't like wind speeds much over 2 miles per hour.) Thus, right at the beginning, one of my basic ideas about olfactory guidance had to be given up at least as it related to fruit flies. The signposts that give them the wind direction are at least partly on the ground.

We could confirm that they were depending on their eyes, by covering the top and bottom of the tunnel with sheets of red Cellophane so that they had only red light to see by. When we did this the moving spots of light lost their effect. Prof. von Frisch in Germany showed long ago that bees' eyes are not sensitive to red light, and we found that fruit flies are similar because with the red Cellophane in place our insects flew very little, and then very close to the floor, and they ignored the moving spots.

This was a rather useful discovery because it meant we could photograph them on red-sensitive panchromatic film without the risk of disturbing them with bright flood lights.

The next experiments we did seemed to be generally consistent with my klinokinetic theory of up-wind guidance. With pure air passing through the tunnel and with an attractive, fermenting-banana smell led into it through a glass tube, the fruit flies took a very complicated and devious course in making their way up to the source of the smell. We sometimes added smoke to the stream of scented air so as to see where it was going, and as far as we could tell the flight pattern seemed to involve a large number of pretty random turns, but with enough system to get them there eventually.

If we gradually slowed down the wind velocity in our tunnel until it stopped entirely, then even though the attractive smell was still present, the flies soon stopped flying and crawled about on the walls. We took this to mean that when there was no wind the 'filaments' in the odour cloud soon smoothed themselves out and the insects no longer got a pulsating odour sensation, and so they no longer had a directional clue even though they might still be aware of something tasty somewhere. Under these conditions, the reasonable thing to do would be to alight and look for it on foot, which was just what they were doing.

So far so good.

We then went to a cruical test of my theory of olfactory guidance. The theory was based on a modification of ordinary klinokinesis and supposed that the smell from a localized source would travel down wind as a tangle of filaments and so be perceived by the insect as an irregular series of pulses or olfactory 'bumps'. The theory could be tested in the following way. If the smell had to be perceived as bumps to produce a directional result, then there should be no directional result if there were no bumps, and there would be none if the wind in our tunnel could be uniformly permeated with the attractive smell. Thus the theory predicted that the flies would ignore a wind that was uniformly permeated with an attractive smell, but they should pay attention again if we generated bumps of a sort by adding a trickle of pure air to the uniformly scented wind. We would create 'negative bumps' and expect to get the same response from the insects as they would normally give to 'positive' ones, because after a pulse or two, there is not much difference between:

. . . pulse, pause, pulse, pause . . .   or   . . . $+ - + - +$ . . .

and,

. . . pause, pulse, pause, pulse . . .   or   . . . $- + - + -$ . . .

We were quite pleased at having thought up this test of the theory and with the help of Mr. Kellogg and Dr. Frizel I arranged to try it.

The first step was to saturate the wind in our tunnel as uniformly as possible with the smell of fermenting bananas. This was not altogether easy and we got some misleadingly encouraging results from the first experiments when the flies seemed to ignore the uniformly scented wind. However, there was a possibility that the scent was too weak rather than too smoothed-out, so we packed the whole end of the wind tunnel with a 2-inch thick layer of foamed plastic soaked in a mush of bananas and yeast, and arranged a mixing chamber with an electric fan ahead of our observation chamber to make sure the smell was distributed uniformly. Then, down at the far end we arranged a wire cage with a door that could be opened suddenly by pulling a string. The idea was that the fruit flies would be kept in the cage while the wind was being started up and the conditions in the tunnel made as uniform as possible, and then they would be released into it. If the theory was correct they should ignore the smell until we made it artificially 'bumpy' by letting in a trickle of pure air.

Everything went well up to the moment when we pulled the string that opened the cage and let loose a cloud of fruit flies into our uniformly scented air—and at that point we were given a complete surprise.

When the flies were released they did not sit around waiting for pulsations of smell to stir them up. On the contrary, they flew straight up wind as fast as they could and settled on the screen at the up-wind end of the tunnel. The photographs showed their flight tracks to be the nearest thing to straight lines we had ever seen an insect fly.

Never was a result more completely unexpected or a working hypothesis so suddenly upset. Whereas I had thought that the randomness was in the insect and that the environment made it systematic, it now appeared that (at least for *Drosophila melanogaster*) the randomness is in the environment, and the insects will behave in a highly systematic manner as long as their environment will let them.

A steady smell-signal evokes in these insects a perfectly steady flight which is directed straight up wind by visual observation of the ground. The experiments showed this without any question and so provided a very firm (if completely unexpected) foundation for the next stage. The experiment gave an answer but not the whole answer because our uniformly perfumed air stream was highly artificial and as unlike the real odour trails as the straight-line flight up the tunnel was unlike their usual intricate path to a piece of banana. We now knew what the insects did when they smelt the attractive scent, but we did not know what they did when they stopped smelling it. Unless we knew this we could not know how the flies kept from over-shooting the source or what they did when they wandered out of the side of the scent stream. With the experimental arrangement we were using it seemed difficult to permeate the air with scent and then suddenly to cut off the scent altogether, and yet that was what we had to do to answer the question.

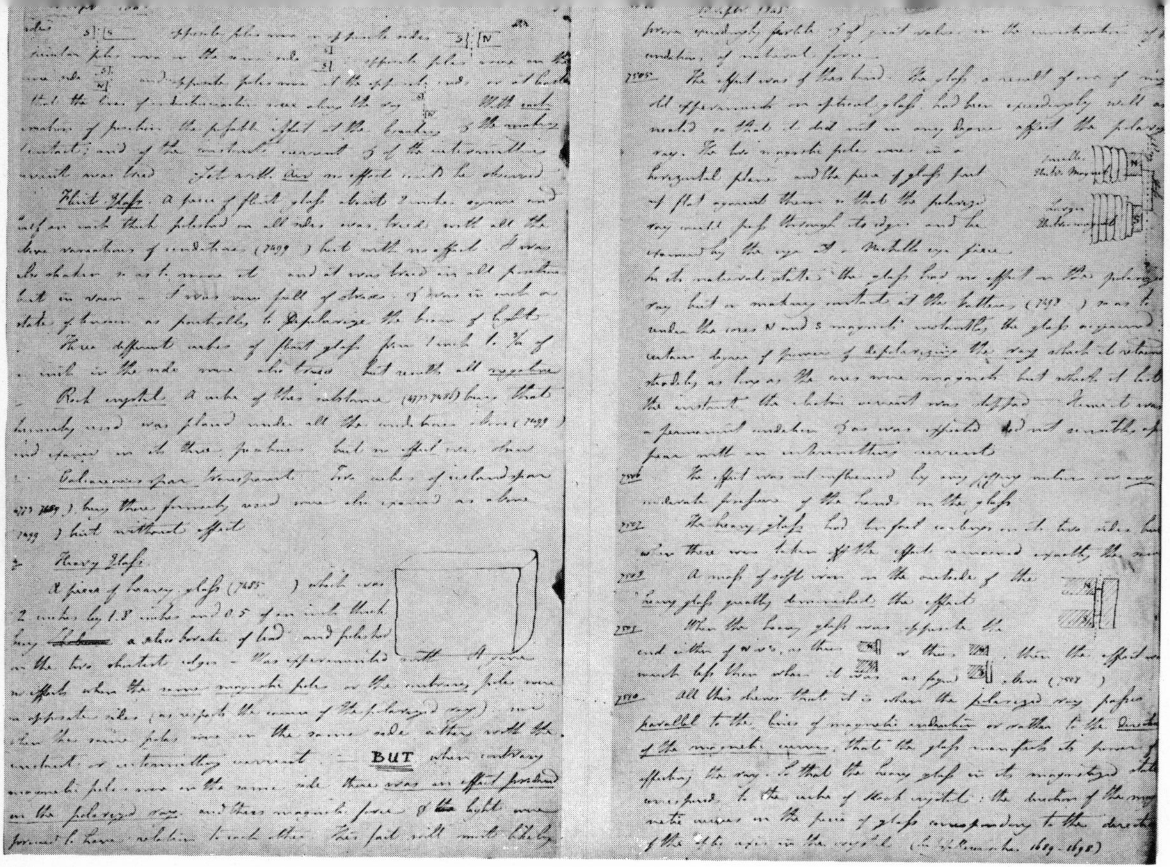

The pages of Faraday's laboratory note book in which he records his discovery of magnetic optical rotation, now known as the 'Faraday Effect'.

Reproduced by kind permission of the Royal Institution

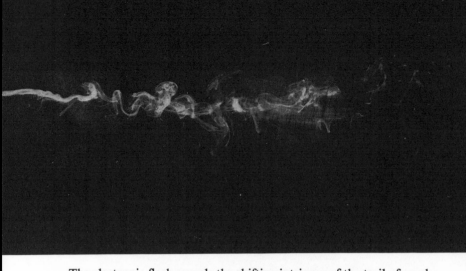

The electronic flash reveals the shifting intricacy of the trail of smoke or odour that a flying insect must follow.

Multiple flashes show the average trail as the mathematical formula describes it. The insect might not agree.

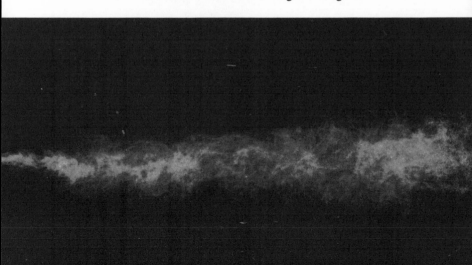

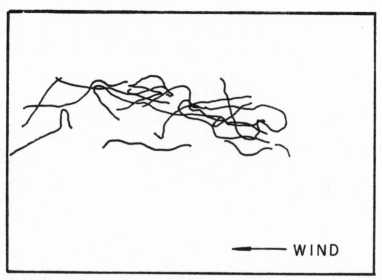

WIND

The upper picture shows tracings from a photograph of fruit flies working their way up wind towards a small source of odour. The various lines are short because the camera recorded only part of the total flight path.

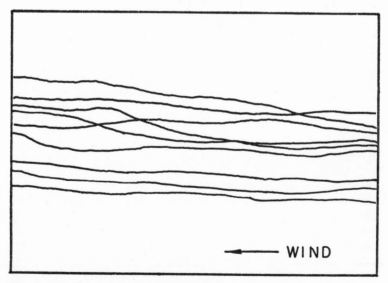

WIND

The lower picture shows tracings from a photograph of fruit flies moving up wind in a uniformly scented air stream.

Fortunately the method turned out to be rather simple. For some of our experiments we had arranged to pass pure air through the tunnel and bleed into it a trickle of scented air through a glass tube. We had found that if this tube projected upward from the bottom or horizontally in from the end of the tunnel we had to tie a bit of gauze over the end to keep the fruit flies from landing on the end of

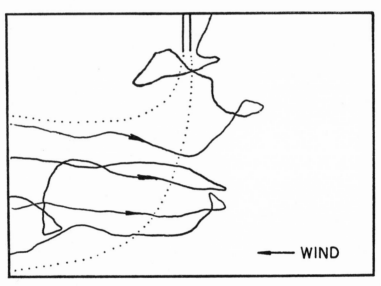

Tracings from a photograph of fruit flies trying to locate the source of an attractive scent injected downwards into an unscented air current.

the tube and crawling into it. Without the gauze they soon plugged the tube.

It occurred to me one day to try inserting the glass tube downward into the wind tunnel so that the trickle of scented air would fall into the air stream and be carried off sideways by the wind. The flies making their way up the trail of scent would then suddenly fly out of the trail and, we hoped, would not see the end of the tube because it would be above them and their eyes were most likely aimed downward. (After all, fermenting fruit is more likely to be found on the ground than hanging on the tree, and it will normally be approached from above or from the side rather than from below.) This simple trick was completely successful and not a single fruit fly ever succeeded in finding and alighting on the end of the glass scent-delivery tube as long as it was projecting downwards.

When we photographed fruit flies following the stream up wind, we found that as before they flew along quite steadily as long as they could smell the scent, but that within a fairly short time of losing it—usually about a fifth of a second—they turned and flew at right angles to the wind direction. They might turn left or right or up or down, but the first reaction was a quick change from up wind to across wind. If they regained the scent they once more turned up wind. If not, they might try one or two more across wind casts before turning back down wind and going back a few inches or maybe a foot or two before making another across wind cast. The result was so prompt and reproducibile that when a lot of fruit flies came up the tunnel at the same time it almost looked as though they were running against some kind of invisible barrier just below and in line with the downward-pointing scent tube. At the same time, the whole process was mechanical as shown by their inability to find the end of the tube when it came down from above.

The reaction time of about a fifth of a second was interesting too because it was longer than the time they normally took to fly from one small 'filament' in the odour cloud to another. With a reaction time that long my klinokinetic mechanism might work a long way from the source but it could hardly work close to it.

Thus by this time my original theory of up-wind guidance was completely demolished so far as fruit flies are concerned. Nevertheless, it had served its purpose, and a very useful purpose. It had led to the planning and carrying out of an experiment designed to test it. We had thought through the consequences of a theory and made a specific and experimentally verifiable prediction. The fact that the prediction was so wholly and completely incorrect was a piece of good fortune that took us off a wrong track and put us on a right one. More often than not, experiments give a much more wishy-washy result.

The fact that we were lucky must not obscure the real moral of this story which is that an incorrect theory that makes you do a fruitful experiment is better than no theory at all. Had we been without any theory of the guidance system we might have spent a long time watching fruit flies puzzling their way up the normal type of fila-mentous odour trail without ending up much wiser. One of the two most important functions of a theory is to stimulate experiments by making predictions that are open to experimental testing. Most of the predictions turn out to be wrong and never get into the published literature—which gives an outsider a false picture of science marching steadily forward from one certainty to the next. I hope I have shown that the truth can be very different.

REFERENCES

G. S. FRAENKEL and D. L. GUNN. *The Orientation of Animals. Kineses, Taxes and Compass Reactions.* Dover Publications, 1961.

F. E. KELLOGG and R. H. WRIGHT. 'The Olfactory Guidance of Flying Insects. III. A Technique for Observing and Recording Flight Paths', *Canadian Entomologist*, **94**, 486–493, 1962.

F. E. KELLOGG, D. E. FRIZEL, and R. H. WRIGHT. 'The Olfactory Guidance of Flying Insects. IV. Drosophila', *Canadian Entomologist*, **94**, 884–888, 1962.

R. H. WRIGHT. 'The Olfactory Guidance of Flying Insects', *Canadian Entomologist*, **90**, 81–89, 1958.

5

Smells and Insects

NOT all insects depend on smells to tell them where to go, what to eat, who to mate with, and where to lay their eggs. Crawling types often seem to rely on the 'feel' or colour of a surface, and many have what appears to be organs of taste on their feet as well as their mouthparts. Temperature, too, and humidity can act as guides, and a few insects respond to vibrations, though it might be too much to say that they can hear. Fleas, for example, may remain dormant until they are activated by the footfalls of an approaching victim, and the stridulations of crickets help them to find each other. Male mosquitoes seem to locate the females at least partly by the sound of their wings—and it has even been suggested that recordings of the noise could be used to draw the males into a trap. (It would be technically rather difficult for Nature to have designed a tympanum that would respond to the audible whine of a mosquito and still be small enough to fit into it. It has therefore been suggested that the male mosquitoes' rather prominent antennae act as sound receptors by vibrating in resonance with the source, somewhat like a tuning fork. This is just one example of the problems introduced by a difference in scale between insects and ourselves.)

The eyes are nearly always important, not only to register wind drift but also to recognize colours and avoid obstacles.

Bees' eyes even have the power to register rather subtle differences in the polarization of light from the sky, and they use this to tell them which way to go regardless of the wind. This is very important to a species that collects honey and brings it home to a hive. If they could only search directly up and down wind they would have a much smaller territory to draw on. Professor von Frisch has found out that a bee which has found a new patch of flowers can tell the other bees how far away it is and in which direction. It is all done in the dark inside the hive and the language they use is not a spoken one. The information is conveyed by a kind of dance on the vertical face of the comb, and the direction of the dance in relation to straight up and down, that is, with respect to the direction of gravity, corresponds to the direction the foragers must take relative to the polarization of the light from the sky when they get outside.

25

Von Frisch's work is one of the most beautiful examples of scientific enquiry I know of, and quite apart from its elegance, the fact that it is entirely non-mathematical makes it especially accessible to the ordinary reader. His writings are classics of contemporary science.

Smell comes into the story right at the end, because after the bees have been told which way to fly and how far, they have to be told which kind of flowers to collect from, and this is done by smell.

Generally speaking, smell is most likely to be important to insects that fly, but it is probably involved somehow in most of the activities of most insects. Of all the sense organs, smell and taste are the least likely to run into scaling difficulties in very small creatures because they operate at the molecular level anyway. Actually, there are only three basic activities that matter: eating, mating, and egg-laying, and so it is interesting to see what kind of smelly chemicals we, or rather the insects, are concerned with.

The smells that lead an insect to its food originate with the food rather than the insect, and so they are not directly related to its body chemistry.

Fruit flies, for example, feed on over-ripe fruit and ignore it while it is green. To be exact, they are not attracted by the part of the fruit they usually eat, which is mostly the juice, but by the chemicals that another organism, the yeast, makes when the fruit begins to go bad. Of the usual products of fermentation, alcohol itself has very little attraction for fruit flies, and it is the chemicals that are formed along with it or are derived from it that are attractive. This is why fruit flies often appear when one is drinking wine, but not when we are drinking distilled liquor which contains the alcohol but not the other fragrant substances.

The fact that wine which is attractive to fruit flies is also considered pleasant or agreeable by people is purely coincidental. In fact, if we separate some of the substances we like best in a pure form the insects pay no attention to them but are drawn instead to others whose odours may not seem particularly strong or pleasant to our noses.

Since many insects serve a very useful purpose as scavengers it is not surprising that the smells associated with putrefaction and decay are highly attractive to them, however repulsive they may be to us. No doubt this, and the economic unimportance of the problem, will serve to explain why so few people have tried to isolate and identify all the specific compounds that attract dung beetles. Such a study might turn out to be unexpectedly useful because it has been shown that some species of African tsetse flies (*Glossina morsitans*

26

and *G. pallidipes*) which attack elephants and cattle, are attracted more by the dung and urine than by the animals themselves. This is another example of the guiding substance coming not from the actual target but from something that normally accompanies or is associated with it.

There is room for much more work on the food attractant substances of various insects. Like horses, insects can be led to the trough, but making them eat may be another matter. Silk worm larvae (*Bombyx mori*) when they are young are attracted to mulberry leaves by a substance, *beta-gamma*-hexenol, and when they are older by an oxidation product of the same compound, *alpha,beta*-hexenal. These substances get them to the leaves, but it requires still another to induce them to bite, and one more to make them swallow!

A mother insect that is looking for a place to lay her eggs is really looking for food for her children if not for herself. The search for suitable ovipositing sites is therefore in the same class with ordinary food searching in that the guiding substance is generated independently of the insect itself.

The egg-laying habits of insects range from the broadcast deposition of mosquito eggs in almost any body of stagnant water to the pinpoint precision of an ichneumon fly which is parasitic on other insects and lays its eggs in their larvae, even when they are hidden deep in the bark of a tree. Incidentally, at the same time that she lays her egg, the ichneumon tags her victim with a repellent smell so that it won't be parasitized twice.

Even when the eggs are broadcast smell can be important. Mosquitoes lay many more eggs in jars of water containing such things as hydrogen sulphide, old yeast infusion, or stale urine, than in a jar of plain tap water used as a control, though this may be as much a matter of taste as smell.

A high degree of precision in choosing an egg-laying site has a real biological value for the following reason. If an insect has grown to maturity, mated, and produced eggs which are ready for laying, it must have survived all the hazards of an uncertain and dangerous world. The first step to success took place when it was born in what proved to be a favourable environment, and so, if it can lay its eggs in a similar environment it may not be the best one possible but it will have been a demonstrably favourable one. As time goes on, the most favourable environments will produce the largest crops of mature offspring until eventually an extraordinary degree of specialization is attained through this process of natural selection.

The specialization appears to be largely fixed in the genetic constitution rather than a learned or imprinted pattern, as shown by

27

the following experiment. The normal prey of the parasite *Nemeritis* is an insect known as *Ephestia*, and it will ignore other insects including the wax moth *Meliphora grisella*. If, however, *Meliphora* larvae are placed in close contact with those of *Ephestia*, the *Nemeritis* parasites can be fooled into laying eggs in the wrong larvae. The eggs develop perfectly, normally, but when the adults emerge they still seem to prefer the original host, *Ephestia*, though they may show a little more attraction towards *Meliphora* than normally reared specimens. This appears to be due to conditioning and could even be regarded as a kind of learning, though their brains are too small to allow much if anything of that sort to take place. These experiments were performed by W. H. Thorpe, and even after several generations of *Nemeritis* had been reared in the 'wrong' host the original preference remained at full strength. In these experiments, the insects were forced on to the wrong host rather than selected for a willingness (however slight) to go there, so there was not much opportunity to build up a genetic preference. Somewhat similar experiments with *Drosophila* fruit flies reared on a medium containing peppermint, which they normally avoid, showed some indication of adaptation after six generations.

Thus the preferences are persistent as well as specialized.

There are bark beetles that will attack only one species of tree, and often only one variety, white pine, for example, but not lodgepole pine. Sometimes a particular kind of tree will be attacked only when it is already over-age, or sick, or weakened in some way. The weakening may be brought about by a fungus or virus disease, or even by the attacks of another kind of insect. Often the difference between the healthy tree and the weakened one is too slight to be seen unless attention is drawn to it by the actions of the insects.

One of the most curious and spectacular cases of this sort is provided by certain wood-boring beetles (*Melanophilia consputa* and *M. atropurpurea*, for example) which are found in large numbers in burned-over timber lands. These insects are strongly attracted by smoke and have been observed running about over the hot surfaces of scorched trees, apparently in search of a suitable place to lay their eggs. When a tree is killed by fire and heat, most of the insects or parasites it harboured will have been killed at the same time, so that the first new attacker to arrive will have a clear field. This may be the original biological advantage that started these 'smoke beetles' on the way to their peculiar specialization. Whatever the reason, they are drawn in large numbers to fires and smoke, and not necessarily to wood smoke. Oil tank fires sometimes collect them in enormous numbers and from surprising distances. A 750,000 barrel fire in

California some years ago collected swarms of them so that they alighted everywhere and even nipped the onlookers. The nearest stand of coniferous trees they could have come from was more than fifty miles away so that their powers of flight are as remarkable as their powers of olfaction.

Tobacco smoke also attracts them and from time to time the spectators at an important football game receive a certain amount of unwelcome attention.

It is not known which constituents of the smoke are attractive, and it might be a matter of some difficulty to find out. Apart from such problems as securing a ready supply of test insects, from the manner of its formation smoke is a highly complex mixture of chemicals. The substances that are present in it depend on what is being burned and also how it is being burned. This may explain occasional reports of outdoor barbecues attracting 'smoke flies' which turn out to be species that normally have no association with fire-damaged trees. On these occasions there is probably some substance present in the smoke that, by pure coincidence, happens to duplicate whatever there is about the normal attractants that the insect perceives.

This kind of thing is probably responsible, too, for occasional reports of insects being attracted in large numbers by unexpected or exotic things like domestic bleach which, on one occasion at least, collected hundreds of beetles of the species *Priacma serrata*, or dry-cleaning fluid containing trichlorethylene which attracted kelp flies (*Coleopa frigida*), or even ordinary kerosene which has been used to trap Mediterranean fruit flies.

It can usually be decided whether insects are assembling in response to a food-attractant or an egg-laying signpost, for the food-attractant will usually collect both males and females and sometimes immature or larval forms as well, while an ovipositing attractant will usually collect females exclusively or predominantly. (However, the attractant may collect the females and they in turn may collect the males, so conclusions must be drawn with care.) Every so often an attractant turns up which collects males exclusively and these are particularly interesting. A male-attracting chemical is normally secreted by the female and so is a product of the insect's own metabolism. Unlike the food or ovipositing attractants which can be almost anything because they originate in the environment, the constitution of the natural sex-attractants that originate within the insects themselves may be expected to throw considerable light on the whole process of olfaction as it relates to insects, and perhaps to the higher animals as well.

We know, or at least we have reason to believe, that the action of these substances is olfactory because of the extremely small concentrations that are sufficient to produce a vigorous response in the male. The amounts are in the 'picogram' range, one picogram being a millionth of a millionth of a gram (10^{-12} gram), which implies roughly the same order of sensitivity as that of our own noses. No other sense, not even taste, comes anywhere near this sensitivity.

The nature of the male's response to these chemicals is usually very characteristic and specific and is related to the mating behaviour. As a result, there is a very sensitive bioassay method available which makes it possible (though by no means easy) to isolate the actual sex-attractant chemical in the pure state and determine its chemical identity. The amount of work involved can be judged by the following example, which is the procedure used by a group of German scientists under the direction of Dr. Butenandt in isolating and purifying the sex-attractant chemical of the silkworm moth, *Bombyx mori*. It is not necessary to understand what was happening at each stage of the chemical manipulation to appreciate the immense patience and painstaking effort that go into a research of this sort.

The starting material was the scent glands from 313,000 female silkworm moths. (Imagine cutting off the abdominal tips from a third of a million moths!) As each was cut off it was stored in light petroleum solvent until finally the whole mass of tips was removed and homogenized in water. The water was then evaporated at low temperature (to avoid 'cooking' the mixture) and the dry residue was extracted with ether. The extract was combined with the material that had been dissolved out in the original petroleum solvent, giving a dark-coloured oil which contained the sex-attractant along with an assortment of unknown contaminants. At each stage of the purification process that followed, whenever the mixture was separated into two or more fractions, a bioassay with male moths was used to show which fraction contained the active substance.

The dark-coloured oil was first shaken up with ether and sodium carbonate solution and the ether layer separated and evaporated to give a residue from which all the acid substances had been extracted by the sodium carbonate. This neutral material was dissolved in methyl alcohol and saponified with potash, after which the mixture was diluted with water and shaken up with ether. The ether layer was separated and the ether evaporated, and the unsaponified residue (which was bioactive) was dissolved in alcohol. The solution was chilled to cause sterols to crystallize, and the alcoholic solution left behind was dried and the solvent evaporated. By treating the residue with pyridine and succinic anhydride, the alcoholic components were converted into succinyl monoesters which were separated by dissolving them in ether, and the ether solution was purified by going through practically all the foregoing steps all over again! This gave a small amount of a residual oily material with a high biological activity, but which was still not pure.

After a further series of purifying operations (which I will not describe—they are even longer than those I have described already) about 4 milligrams—a very small drop—of an oily liquid was left which was the pure sex-attractant and which possessed an almost unbelievably high biological activity. A millionth of a gram (10^{-6} gram) is called a microgram, and a millionth of a microgram (10^{-12} gram) is called a picogram. In this case, a millionth of a picogram (10^{-18} gram) in one cubic centimetre of petroleum solvent was enough to excite the male silkworm moth. The systematic name of the moth is *Bombyx mori*, and so the sex-attractant chemical was named 'Bombycol'.

So far so good, but there was still a long way to go.

Isolating the pure sex-attractant chemical was only the first step (though a very necessary one) on the way to determining its chemical constitution. It could be estimated approximately that the molecular weight was something over 200, which would indicate that the molecule was made up of 40 to 50 atoms. Just as a 'Meccano' set containing fifty pieces can be used to make a great many models, so a set of 50 atoms can be put together in a great many ways. The problem of establishing which of these possibilities was actually embodied in the substance Bombycol has now become a routine type of operation (though never an easy one) for organic chemists, and in due course the constitution was shown to be,

$$CH_3—CH_2—CH_2—CH{=}CH—CH{=}CH—(CH_2)_7—CH_2—OH$$

This is what is called a 'structural formula'. It is a sort of schematic 'wiring diagram' of the molecule, showing the kinds of atoms it is made of and which ones are joined to which. It is not a picture of the molecule any more than the wiring diagram of a radio set is a picture of the actual finished receiver, but it is more useful than a picture for chemical purposes because it shows how the molecule can be made.

In this case, the wiring diagram as written does not tell the whole story because, while it shows which atoms are joined and by what kinds of bonds, it does not tell how the parts are arranged in three-dimensional space. For the structure of Bombycol there are at least four possible configurations which come about as a result of the fact

31

that two pairs of carbon atoms are joined by double bonds. If we abbreviate the structure to:

$$A—CH=CH—CH=CH—B$$

the four possibilities can be schematically represented like this:

$$
(1)\quad
\begin{array}{c}
A—C—H \\
\| \\
H—C—C—H \\
\| \\
B—C—H
\end{array}
\qquad
(2)\quad
\begin{array}{c}
H—C—A \\
\| \\
H—C—C—H \\
\| \\
H—C—B
\end{array}
$$

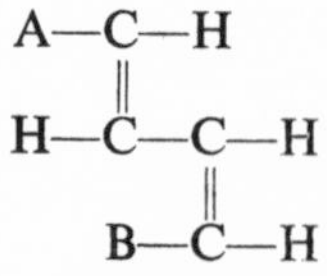

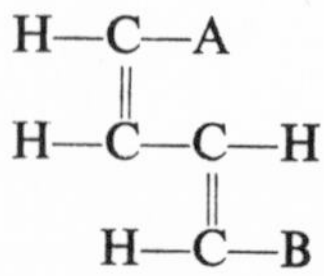

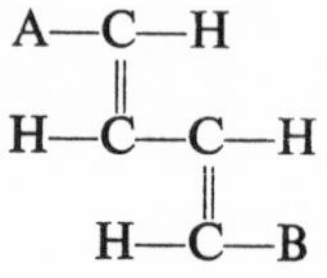

$$
(3)\quad
\begin{array}{c}
A—C—H \\
\| \\
H—C—C—H \\
\| \\
H—C—B
\end{array}
\qquad
(4)\quad
\begin{array}{c}
H—C—A \\
\| \\
H—C—C—H \\
\| \\
B—C—H
\end{array}
$$

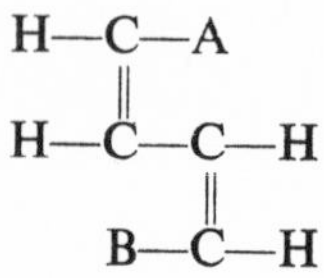

There are several ways of deciding which of these arrangements is Bombycol, but the surest is to make all four structures synthetically and see which of the four matches Bombycol in all its properties. The four compounds were therefore synthesized, not once but three times by three different methods so as to make sure, and it turned out that Bombycol has the structure (1).

The biological activity of the other three was tested. Structure (2) had an even stronger effect than the natural Bombycol, whereas (3) and (4) were much weaker. This is not unusual with biologically active chemicals in general and odourous ones particularly. Quite slight changes in the structure or configuration will sometimes make a vast difference in their effects, though the opposite is also true and similar effects can be produced by compounds that are apparently very different.

I have gone into this story of the German work on Bombycol at some length so as to show the effort and labour that lie behind a simple statement that, 'The sex-attractant chemical of the silkworm moth has been isolated and shown to be . . .' It will explain why only a few such sex-attractant chemicals have been isolated and identified so far.

Very recently, however, an easier way has been found to isolate these substances. Dr. Jacobson and his associates in the U.S. Department of Agriculture set up a battery of metal containers (actually milk cans) in which they kept about ten thousand virgin female cockroaches (*Periplaneta americana*). The insects were replaced as required, and the experiment went on for nine months. During the whole of that time purified air was drawn through the containers and then through a trap which was cooled with solid carbon dioxide ('dry ice') and containing a little dilute hydrochloric acid. In this way they collected the volatile sex-attractant and a few other volatile substances released by the cockroaches, but the material was much simpler to work up than the mixture they would have had starting with actual tissues. This made the purification much easier.

The sex-attractant they isolated was biologically active at very low concentrations so that a comparatively few molecules of it produced a most intense excitement in the males, making them raise their wings in a peculiar and very characteristic way. Its chemical structure has been worked out and is represented by the formula:

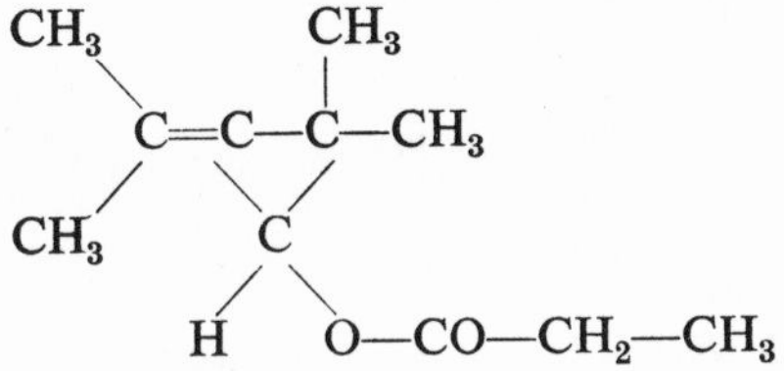

$$
\begin{array}{c}
CH_3 \qquad\qquad CH_3 \\
| \qquad\qquad\quad | \\
C=C-C-CH_3 \\
CH_3 \qquad C \\
H \qquad O-CO-CH_2-CH_3
\end{array}
$$

The wing flapping response of the sexually excited males may not be altogether pointless or merely a means of attracting attention. It is a fairly common response with more than one kind of insect, and one suggestion is that it carries a scent from the male towards the female. Where there is a close physical similarity between two insect species, a male scent that made the female receptive would be useful in preventing cross-mating. There is some evidence that this really happens. E. Mayr, for example, found that cross-mating never took place between *Drosophila pseudoobscura* and *Drosophila persimilis* under natural conditions, but that if the antennae of the *females* were removed, the two species mated almost at random. A similar tendency to cross-mate was observed by G. Streisinger with *Drosophila pseudoobscura* and *Drosophila melanogaster* when the females were etherized.

The practical importance of this kind of observation has still to be recognized and exploited.

REFERENCES

M. D. ATKINS. 'An Interesting Attractant for *Priacma serrata* (Lec.)', *Canadian Entomologist*, **89**, 214–219, 1957. (Attraction by bleach.)

C. T. BRUES. 'Vespid Wasps (*Eumenes curvata*) Attracted to (cigarette) Smoke', *Psyche*, Camb. Mass., **57**, 114–115, 1950.

A. BUTENANDT. (Active Substances from Insects.) *Naturwissenschaften*, **46**, 461–471, 1959.

A. BUTENANDT, R. BECKMANN, D. STAMM, and E. HECKER. (On the Sexual Attractant of the Silkworm Moth, Bombyx mori. Purification and Constitution.) *Z. Naturforsch*, **14b**(4), 283–284, 1959.

A. BUTENANDT, R. BECKMANN, and E. HECKER. (Sexual Attractant of the Silk Moth. I. Biological Testing and Isolation of the Pure Sexual Attractant, Bombycol.) *Z. Physiol. Chem.*, **324**, 71–83, 1961.

A. BUTENANDT, R. BECKMANN, and D. STAMM. (Sexual Attractant of the Silk Moth. II. Constitution and Configuration of Bombycol.) *Z. Physiol. Chem.*, **324**, 84–87, 1961.

A. BUTENANDT and E. HECKER. (Synthesis of Bombycol, the Sexual Bait Substance of the Mulberry Silk Moth and its Geometrical Isomers.) *Angew. Chem.*, **73**, 349–353, 1961.

J. A. CHAPMAN. 'Field Studies on Attack Flight and Log Selection by the Ambrosia Beetle, *Trypodendron lineatum* (Oliv.)', *Canadian Entomologist*, **94**, 74–92, 1962.

T. W. CHORLEY. '*Glossina pallidipes* Austen Attracted by the Scent of Cattle-Dung and Urine', *Proc. Roy. Ent. Soc., London*, **23**, 9–11, 1948.

V. G. DETHIER. *Chemical Insect Attractants and Repellants.* Blakiston, Philadelphia, 1947.

K. VON FRISCH. *Bees: Their Vision, Chemical Senses and Language.* Cornell University Press, 1950.

Y. HAMAMURA. 'Food Selection by Silkworm Larvae', *Nature*, **183**, 1746–1747, 1959.

M. JACOBSON, M. BEROZA, and R. T. YAMAMOTO. 'Isolation and Identification of the Sex Attractant of the American Cockroach', *Science*, **139**, 48–49, 1963.

E. G. LINSLEY. 'Attraction of *Melanophilia* Beetles by Fire and Smoke', *J. Econ. Ent.*, **36**, 341–342, 1943. See also, E. C. DYKE. 'Buprestid Swarming', *Pan-Pacific Ent.*, **3**, 41, 1926.

W. H. THORPE. 'Further Experiments on Olfactory Conditioning in a Parasitic Insect. The Nature of the Conditioning Process', *Proc. Roy. Soc.*, **126**, 370–397, 1938.

W. H. THORPE. 'Further Studies on Pre-imaginal Olfactory Conditioning of Insects', *Proc. Roy. Soc.*, **127**, 424–433, 1939.

C. M. WILLIAMS. 'Laboratory Procedures in Studies of the Chemical Control of Insects. Dry Cleaning Fluid as an Attractant for the Kelp Fly', *Publ. Amer. Assn. Adv. Sci.*, **20**, 174, 1943.

G. WISHART, G. R. VAN SICKLE, and D. F. RIORDAN. 'Orientation of the Males of *Aedes aegypti* (L) to Sound', *Canadian Entomologist*, **94**, 613–626, 1962.

NOTE. As this book is written in English, the titles of articles written in other languages have been rendered into English, but are enclosed in brackets rather than quotation marks.

6

Sex and Insects

A SEX-ATTRACTANT scent that collects male Mediterranean fruit flies (*Ceratitis capitata*) has been discovered by a different route. This insect is a pest of citrus fruits and it is important to have early warning of an outbreak and also to be able to make a census of the infestation as a check on the success of control operations. Sex attractants are especially useful for this because they are so specific. In March, 1956, it was found, largely by trial and error, that angelica seed oil has a powerful attraction for male Medflies. An extensive trapping programme showed that there was a real use for the attractant in fighting the outbreak—but it also used up the whole world supply of angelica seed oil, which in fact amounted to only a few hundred pounds. An intensive search was therefore made for substitute attractants, preferably ones that could be made synthetically and in quantity.

To save time, the actual sex-attractant chemical secreted by the females was not isolated and identified first as was done with the silkworm moth. Instead, a random selection of several thousand organic chemicals was put through a screening process to see whether any of them might accidentally prove to be attractive. This turned up some leads which were followed up intensively with the result that several very good synthetic baits for male Medflies were discovered in a surprisingly short time. It is most unlikely that they actually duplicate the chemical structure of the natural attractant which has still not been identified, but for practical purposes this does not matter. A compound which was named 'Siglure' was produced which was nearly as attractive as angelica seed oil and much cheaper. It had the constitution:

35

More than thirty variants of this structure were also synthesized (the work was done by scientists of the U.S. Department of Agriculture in several laboratories) and about a quarter of them were attractive to some degree. For practical use a chemical lure must be attractive and not too volatile or it will evaporate out of a trap too quickly. There are several other properties it must have, including low cost. The variants of Siglure that were the same in the ring part of the molecule but differed in the part of the side chain beyond the —O— atom, all tended to be somewhat attractive but differed in volatility and staying power.

The first lots to be made commercially were rather disappointing because they were much less active than the laboratory specimens. It turned out that, as was the case with Bombycol, there was more than one way of arranging the parts of the molecule in space. To show this in a diagram, we must suppose that we are looking at the ring-shaped part of the molecule from one side, more or less edge on, in which case the groups attached to the ring can be on the same side of it (what is called the 'cis-configuration') or on opposite sides (giving the 'trans-configuration').

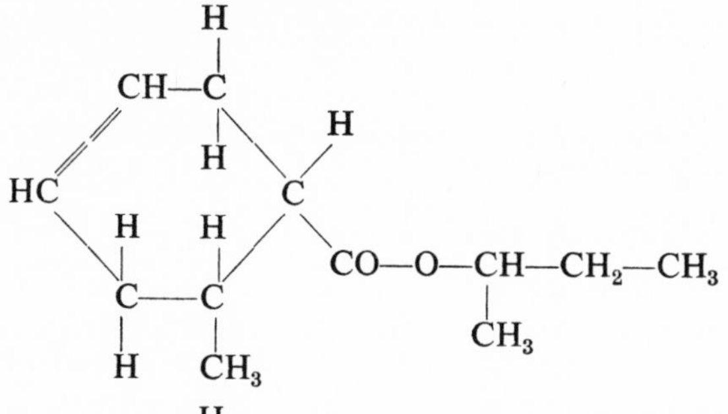

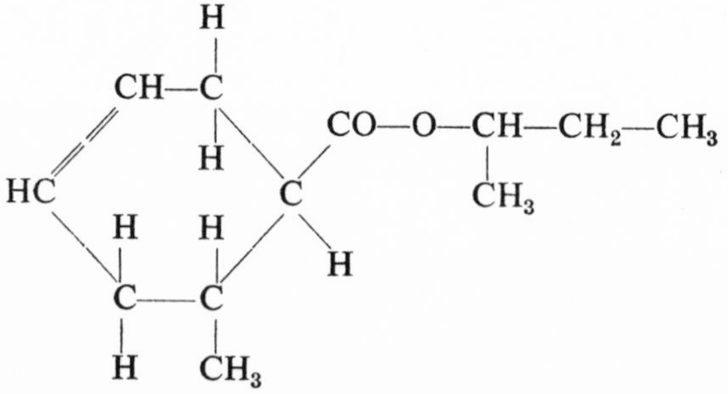

These two forms (or 'isomers') were prepared synthetically, and it then appeared that the *trans*- form is the biologically active one, and that the *cis*- form is quite unattractive to male Medflies. The first

Collecting the Sex Attractant of the American Cockroach

These milk cans contained ten thousand virgin female *Peri-planeta Americana*. The volatile sex attractant was swept out in a current of air and collected in a cold trap. It took nine months to recover 12·2 milligrams.

Photograph by the Pesticide Chemicals Research Branch of the U.S. Department of Agriculture

Male *Periplaneta Americana* showing the characteristic mating response to the pure sex attractant chemical which has been applied as an invisible film to the glass slide.

Photograph by the Pesticide Chemicals Research Branch of the U.S. Department

lots of the commercial product contained a proportion of this form. When the method of manufacture was changed to correct this, the product was satisfactory though not perfect. There is always room for improvement.

In this case, the improvement took the form of a change in the ring part of the molecule, which was modified by adding a hydrogen atom and a chlorine or bromine atom at the double bond, to give a product known as 'Medlure' which is more attractive and longer lasting than Siglure. Taking into account the two possible carbon atoms for the chlorine (or bromine) atom to attach itself to, and the further possibility that it may lie above or below the plane of the ring, there are four possible 'trans-' configurations for Medlure, one of them being represented diagrammatically like this:

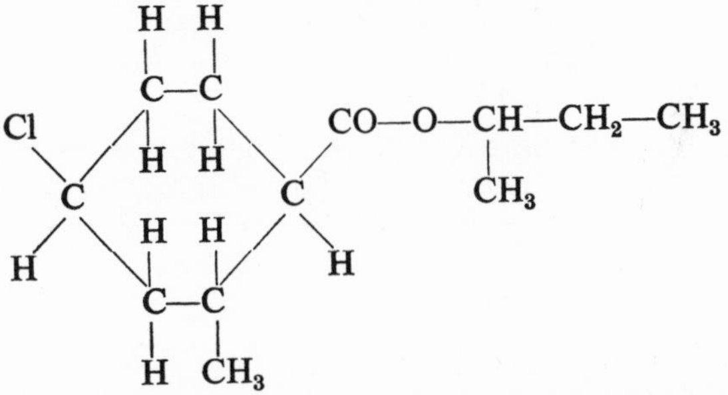

Medlure

(You may want to try your hand at writing down the structures of the other three 'trans-' configurations and the four corresponding 'cis-' forms.) It is not known which form is commercial Medlure. It may be a mixture.

The game of varying the part of the molecule attached to the —O— atom was gone through once more and forty-six variants were made. One was enough better than Medlure in attractancy, though not in persistency, to be given the name 'Trimedlure'. The difference between it and Medlure is rather slight:

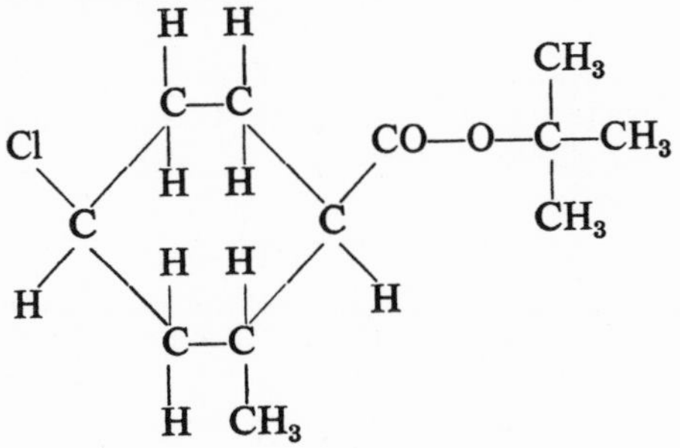

Trimedlure

37

Another expensive pest is the melon fly (*Dacus curcurbitae*), which is found in Hawaii and elsewhere. In an initial study, like the one that led to the development of Siglure and the Medlures, more than a thousand miscellaneous chemicals were screened for ability to attract the male melon flies, and a few were found to be attractive. The two best ones were:

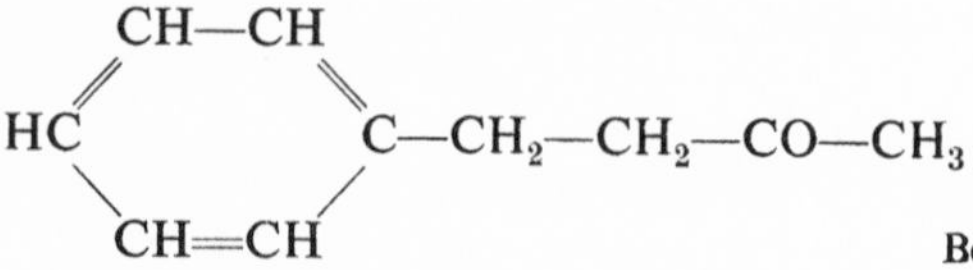

$$HC\underset{CH=CH}{\overset{CH-CH}{\diagup \diagdown}}C-CH_2-CH_2-CO-CH_3$$

Benzyl acetone

and

$$CH_3-O-C\underset{CH=CH}{\overset{CH-CH}{\diagup \diagdown}}C-CH_2-CH_2-CO-CH_3$$

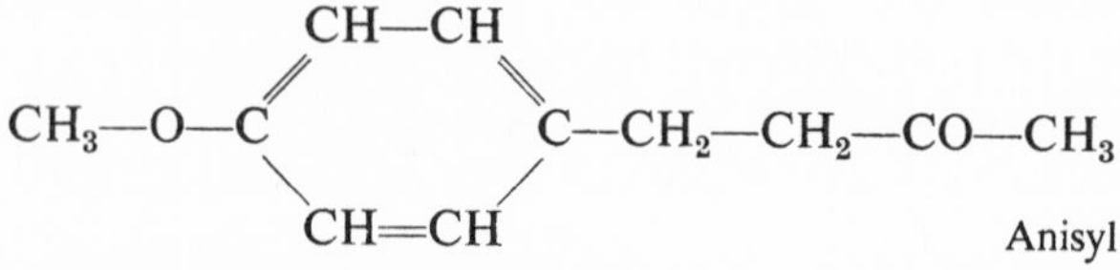

Anisyl acetone

In the usual way, the changes were rung on these structures (more than three thousand compounds were tested and a few hundred of them gave positive responses) with the usual rather puzzling results. For example, this one, which is rather similar to anisyl acetone is not at all attractive to the melon fly:

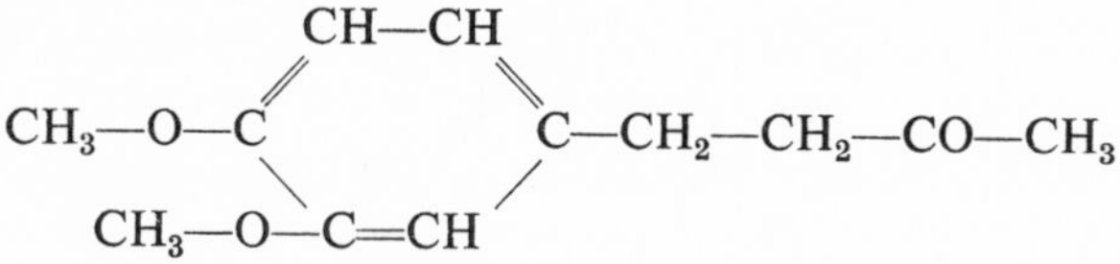

$$CH_3-O-C\underset{CH_3-O-C=CH}{\overset{CH-CH}{\diagup \diagdown}}C-CH_2-CH_2-CO-CH_3$$

On the other hand, this one is so highly attractive as to be given the name, 'Cue-Lure':

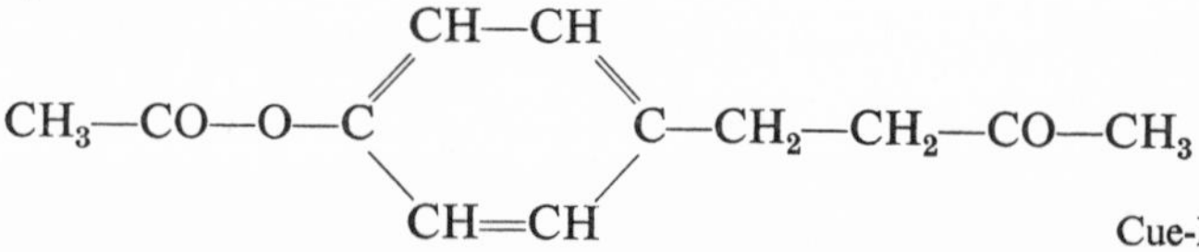

$$CH_3-CO-O-C\underset{CH=CH}{\overset{CH-CH}{\diagup \diagdown}}C-CH_2-CH_2-CO-CH_3$$

Cue-Lure

It is not known why such small changes in the structure should affect the biological activity of these compounds. For the time being, 'it is just one of those things . . .' What makes it all still more puzzling is the probability that these compounds do not in any way duplicate the actual structure of the natural attractant as it is secreted by the female melon fly. From a practical point of view this does not matter, but from the long-term understanding of the chemistry of the natural sex-attractants, it would be interesting to know what is the common thread that gives them their activity.

Another attractant that has recently been studied with success is that of the Gypsy moth (*Porthetria dispar*). Marked males have been known to find females from distances of over two miles, so that the lure is evidently very powerful. Like Medlure and Cue-Lure, this problem was investigated by the group of scientists in the U.S. Department of Agriculture (as well as groups elsewhere). The abdominal tips from several hundred thousand female gypsy moths were cut off and extracted, and the extract was worked up in the same general way as the extract from the silkworm moths described in the last chapter. The final result had the following structure and was the natural sex-attractant:

$$\overset{\text{'}cis\text{-'}}{CH_3-(CH_2)_5-CH-CH=CH-(CH_2)_5-CH_2-OH}$$
$$\underset{O-CO-CH_3}{|}$$

As soon as this had been worked out it was seen that a closely similar substance could be synthesized very easily starting with a compound called ricinoleic acid which is readily obtainable from castor oil. The substitute is the same except that the main chain of carbon atoms is longer by two $-CH_2-$ groups which are inserted to the right of the side-chain. This substance is actually more active than the natural attractant. As little as 10 picograms (10^{-5} micrograms or 10^{-11} grams) in a trap will collect large numbers of males in the field, and in a laboratory bioassay as little as a millionth of a picogram (or 10^{-18} grams) is active. This synthetic variant of the natural lure was named 'Gyplure'.

Because of the double bond in the molecule, both the natural attractant and the synthetic Gyplure can exist in *cis*- and *trans*- forms. It has been shown that only the *cis*- form is active. If the chain is made still longer, extending it by two more $-CH_2-$ groups again to the right of the side-chain, the activity is considerably diminished, and it decreases also if the side chain is changed to

$$-O-CO-CH_2-CH_2-CH_3$$

or

$$-O-CO-CH_2-CH_2-CH_2-CH_3$$

Once more, the reason why the activity is affected by these changes is not known.

One of the most recent insect sex-attractant chemicals to be identified is that of the queen bee (*Apis mellifera*). Unlike the female Gypsy moth which cannot fly and must await the arrival of a male, the queen bee makes a mating flight and meets the drone in mid air.

The technical problems to be solved by two middling-small insects moving freely in three dimensions and coming together from starting places that may be half a mile apart can best be compared with those of two astronauts rendezvousing in outer space. Nevertheless, the problems are solved with the aid of an attracting odour which has now been shown to consist mainly if not entirely of a compound with the structure:

$$CH_3—CO—CH_2—CH_2—CH_2—CH_2—CH_2—CH\!=\!CH—CO—OH$$

The bioassays in this case were unusually difficult because the drones will not pay any attention to the queen bee if she is less than about 15 feet above the ground. The tests had therefore to be carried out in the open air using toy balloons to support queen bees tethered on nylon filaments, or bits of filter paper impregnated with chemicals to be tested, and the drones were watched from the ground with binoculars. The attractant chemical is unusual in that it is secreted in the mouthparts of the queen bee which has unusually large mandibular glands.

Natural sex attractant chemicals, or synthetic substitutes like Medlure, have a tremendous potential importance because they are so highly specific in their effect. This follows from their natural role which is to see to it that the right kind of males, and only the right kind of males, are attracted to the females to mate with them. They are so specific that they can be used to take a census or survey an area, and what is likely to be more and more important as time goes on, they can be mixed with poisons and used to kill off members of one, and only one, species selectively. In this way, honey bees and beneficial parasites can be spared systematically rather than killed indiscriminately as they are when a poison is sown broadcast.

Quite recently a still more interesting possibility has appeared.

Certain chemicals have been found that have the power to render insects sexually sterile without killing them. If a sex-attractant chemical can be used to bring males into contact with such a chemical, and if the males are then allowed to go about their business, each one that finds and mates with a female will, in a biological sense 'kill' her, because an individual that does not reproduce itself is as good as dead. These 'chemi-sterilants' are evidently very powerful chemicals, even more so than many of the ordinary insecticides, and it would not do to spread them around as freely as insecticides have been distributed in the past. If they can be used in conjunction with a species-specific attractant (usually but not necessarily a sex attractant) they can be kept well away from the property they are to protect, and so made much safer.

40

The development of these powerful and highly specific lures is being somewhat delayed by the very fact that they are so powerful. A little goes such a long way! For example, the U.S. Department of Agriculture uses only about 1000 lb. of Medfly attractant a year, and 100 lb. of synthetic Gypsy moth attractant is enough to service 30,000 traps for a year. This means that the market for these chemicals is pretty small, and chemical companies are reluctant to spend large sums on research and development of compounds that will not be required in ton- or tank-car lots. Most of the research on them has therefore to be done in Government or University Laboratories where 'science for its own sake' is allowed and encouraged.

I think this situation is likely to change rather quickly as soon as we learn to think of the attractive properties of these chemicals as secondary, and to consider them primarily as recognition signals. When we do that, a new and important way of using them might appear.

By scattering a chemical recognition scent (or an acceptable imitation of it) broadcast on the same scale that insecticides are often used today, we could expect to saturate the sensory mechanisms of the relevant insects to a point where they could neither locate nor recognize their partners, and their normal responses would be so confused and over-stimulated that they would no longer be able to mate effectively. In the language of information theory, the 'noise-to-signal' ratio would become so large that effective communication would cease between the sexes. Such a method of using these chemicals would have the advantage that it would usually be specific to one insect species at a time, and furthermore, the chemicals involved would not be toxic. This is particularly important in view of the growing concern over the contamination of the environment by persistent insecticides.

Because of the very great biological potency of these substances, the amounts required to 'saturate' an infested area would not be prohibitive, but should be enough to create a mass market that would interest the chemical manufacturers.

Recently scientists at the University of Wisconsin set out wire traps coated with a sticky adhesive and each baited with one female pine sawfly (*Diprion similis*). Some of the traps caught no males, perhaps because the females in them were not trying. However, eight traps (each with only one female) caught an average of one thousand males apiece, the lowest being 542 and the highest 1706; and one uniquely marvellous female collected eleven thousand males in eight days—during the last three of which she was dead!

REFERENCES

B. H. ALEXANDER, M. BEROZA, T. A. ODA, L. F. STEINER, D. H. MIYASHITA, and W. C. MITCHELL. 'Insect Attractants, Development of Male Melon Fly Attractants', *J. Agr. Food. Chem.*, **10**, 270–275, 1962.

M. BEROZA, B. H. ALEXANDER, L. F. STEINER, W. C. MITCHELL, and D. H. MIYASHITA. 'New Synthetic Lures for the Male Melon Fly', *Science*, **131**, 1044–1045, 1960.

M. BEROZA, N. GREEN, S. I. GERTLER, L. F. STEINER, and D. H. MIYASHITA. 'New Attractants for the Mediterranean Fruit Fly', *J. Agr. Food. Chem.*, **9**, 361–365, 1961.

A. B. BORKOVEC. 'Sexual Sterilization of Insects by Chemicals', *Science*, **137**, 1034–1037, 1962.

J. E. CASIDA, H. C. COPPEL, and T. WATANABE. 'Purification and Potency of the Sex Attractant from the Introduced Pine Sawfly, *Diprion Similis*', *J. Econ. Ent.*, **56** (1), 18–24, Feb., 1963.

H. C. COPPEL, J. E. CASIDA, and W. C. DAUTERMAN. 'Evidence for a Potent Sex Attractant in the Introduced Pine Sawfly, *Diprion Similis*', *Ann. Ent. Soc. Amer.*, **53**, 510–512, 1960.

N. E. GARY. 'Chemical Mating Attractants in the Queen Honey Bee', *Science*, **136**, 773–774, 1962.

S. I. GERTLER, L. F. STEINER, W. C. MITCHELL, and W. F. BARTHEL. 'Esters of 6-Methyl-3-cyclohexene-1-carboxylic acid as Attractants for the Mediterranean Fruit Fly', *J. Agr. Food. Chem.*, **6**, 592–594, 1958.

N. GREEN and M. BEROZA. 'Cis-trans Isomers of 6-Methyl-3-cyclohexene-1-carboxylic acid, and their sec.-Butyl Esters', *J. Org. Chem.*, **24**, 761–764, 1959.

M. JACOBSON. 'Synthesis of a Highly Potent Gypsy Moth Sex Attractant', *J. Org. Chem.*, **25**, 2074, 1960.

M. JACOBSON, M. BEROZA, and W. A. JONES. 'Insect Sex Attractants. I. The Isolation, Identification, and Synthesis of the Sex Attractant of the Gypsy Moth', *J. Am. Chem. Soc.*, **83**, 4819–4824, 1961.

M. JACOBSON and W. A. JONES. 'Insect Sex Attractants. II. Synthesis of a Highly Potent Gypsy Moth Sex Attractant and Some Related Compounds', *J. Org. Chem.*, **27**, 2523–2524, 1962.

E. MAYR. 'The Role of the Antennae in the Mating Behaviour of Female Drosophila', *Evolution*, **4**, 149–154, 1950.

L. F. STEINER, D. H. MIYASHITA, and L. D. CHRISTENSON. 'Angelica Oils as Mediterranean Fruit Fly Lures', *J. Econ. Ent.*, **50**, 505, 1957.

L. F. STEINER, W. C. MITCHELL, N. GREEN, and M. BEROZA. 'Effect of Cis-trans Isomerism on the Potency of an Insect Attractant', *J. Econ. Ent.*, **51**, 921–922, 1958.

G. STREISINGER. 'Experiments on Sexual Isolation in Drosophila. IX. Behaviour of Males with Etherized Females', *Evolution*, **2**, 187–188, 1948.

R. H. WRIGHT. 'Molecular Vibration and Insect Sex Attractants', *Nature*, **198**, 455–459, 1963.

7

How Keen is the Nose?

THE substances that appear to have very powerful smells to insects often seem faint to us, which leads some people to think that insects' noses are much keener than ours. This would be true only if all creatures were equipped to smell the same things, and there is no reason why they should be. In fact, the sensitivity of the human nose is by no means contemptible. Of course, if it is treated with contempt, if it is ignored and its power wasted, or if it is embalmed with smoke or anaesthetized with gasoline fumes or corroded with chemicals, it will not amount to much. A professional smeller can do some wonderful things, whether he is a perfumer, or a food taster, or an aboriginal savage who finds his nose nearly as useful as his eyes in tracking down his game. Blind people sometimes cultivate their sense of smell so as to make it a most useful supplement to their ears and fingers, and it is strange that they have not been encouraged and trained to do this more often.

In order to perceive a smell, we must draw the odourized air into our noses, and for best results the air has to be actively sniffed. The sensitive area is in the upper part of the nasal passage, in what is called the olfactory cleft, and in ordinary breathing most of the inspired air by-passes it. The smallest concentration of odourous material that will generate a sensation is called the threshold concentration. It may be expressed in various ways: as grams of odourous substance per litre, or sometimes as the number of individual molecules in a volume such as 50 c.c.—which is sometimes referred to as 'one sniff'.

Threshold measurements have been made in various ways and with various degrees of precision. One system, called the blast injection technique, was developed and used extensively by C. A. Elsberg. It uses an atomizer to spray air containing a known concentration of scent right up into the olfactory cleft. This is distinctly unnatural and calls for a rather tolerant and co-operative subject. The alternative is some sort of natural sniffing and is probably preferable, though harder to control precisely.

Using the sniffing technique, Neuhaus has measured the threshold of perception for several chemicals by man and also by the dog, and these are some of his figures:

	Threshold concentration (molecules per cu. cm.)	
Substance	Dog	Man
Acetic acid .	2×10^5	5×10^{13}
Butyric acid .	9×10^3	7×10^9
Ethyl mercaptan .	2×10^5	4×10^8
Alpha ionone .	1×10^5	3×10^8

These are averages, and there is usually considerable variation between different smellers whether they be men or dogs. For example, in a group of twelve dogs (ten German shepherds, one Rottweiler, and one Hovawart) the threshold varied from 1·7 to 12×10^3 molecules per cu. cm. Neuhaus' results seem to fall into two main groups: smells like acetic and butyric acid which the dog can perceive at concentrations a million times lower than we can, and smells like mercaptan and ionone where his threshold is only about a thousand times better. It seems likely that where the sensitivity is a million times better the dog is equipped to smell something that we do not. When there is only a factor of a thousand between us, it is likely that we and the dog have similar receptors but that the odourous molecules get to the dog's more easily than to ours. Very recently, deVries and Stuiver have tried to estimate the absolute sensitivity of the human nose. To do this, they started with the observed threshold concentrations and estimated what fraction of a 50 cu. cm. sniff would actually pass into and through the olfactory cleft, and out of this volume, how many molecules would actually make contact with the end organ.

They came to the conclusion that something less than eight individual molecules on a single nerve ending will trigger an impulse in it, and that about forty nerve endings have to co-operate before a sensation will actually be perceived. Since it is unlikely that this can be improved on very much even by a dog, we can conclude that once the odourous air reaches the sensitive surface in our noses, and provided the smell is one we are equipped to smell, our sensitivity is as good as the dog's. Where the dog wins is in having better access of air to the sensitive area, and a sensitive area that is sensitive to a wider spectrum of sensations, and in having a brain that is better equipped to register, remember, and interpret the information its nose brings to it.

While we are on the subject of threshold concentrations, let us look at what is known about the powers of some other creatures.

Insects we have already considered, and where they are sensitive at all they seem to be about as sensitive as the dog or the man.

Goff studied the threshold sensitivities of rats in an interesting way. He trained them to press a bar in an inhalation chamber in response to an odour, and then diluted it until they no longer responded correctly. In this way he found that the threshold for pentane was 1×10^8 molecules per c.c.

W. Lindemann investigated the way hedgehogs (*Erinaceus europaeus*) react to smells and found that they could detect an edible beetle one metre (39 inches) away, and a hostile dog at nine metres (about 30 feet).

It is generally considered that birds have relatively undeveloped smell senses, but in fact there has not been very much work done on them. Humming-birds appear to rely entirely on sight to locate a flower, but W. J. Michelsen trained male white Carneaux pigeons to recognize *sec*-butyl acetate and *iso*-octane. B. G. Bang showed by dissection that at least three species of bird have highly developed olfactory organs, and Owre and Northington confirmed it by behaviour studies with one of them, *Cathartes aura* (L). This is the North American turkey vulture which feeds on carrion, and they showed that it could locate pieces of meat hidden under a layer of leaves. Probably a scavenger like the vulture needs a sense of smell more than a humming-bird does. On the whole, the smell sense in birds has been rather neglected.

Fish have been given rather more attention, for one thing because of their remarkable ability in some cases to find their way back to the stream where they were born.

A patent has been granted to two American scientists for the use of potassium phenyl acetate to frighten away fish without poisoning them, by adding the chemical to water at concentrations as low as one part in ten million million (1 in 10^{13}).

D. M. Stevens in a study of some West Indian fish found that water extracts of mammalian tissue or of live plankton were perceived by the fish at concentrations of about one in a thousand million (1 in 10^9). Some of the substances they respond to were identified as creatinine, lactic acid, and glutamic acid:

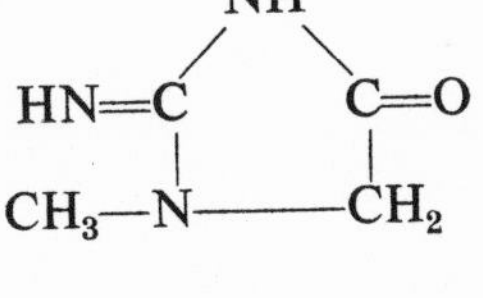

$$\begin{array}{c} NH \\ / \ \backslash \\ HN{=}C \qquad C{=}O \\ | \qquad\qquad | \\ CH_3{-}N{-}{-}{-}{-}CH_2 \end{array}$$

Creatinine

$$CH_3—CHOH—COOH$$ Lactic acid

$$HOOC—CH_2—CH_2—CH—COOH$$
$$\underset{NH_2}{|}$$
Glutamic acid

(Glutamic acid is, of course, the basis of the well-known food additive, monosodium glutamate.)

When Stevens blinded the fish they responded like unoperated ones, which suggests that they use their sense of smell to locate food when the water is too dark or too muddy for them to see it.

The eel (*Anguilla anguilla* (L)), whose amazing migrations are another story, appears to have remarkable olfactory powers. H. Teichmann trained European eels to differentiate between synthetic odours like *beta*-phenyl ethyl alcohol (it smells like roses to us) or *alpha*-ionone (violets), and he measured the threshold concentrations as being about 1 part in 3×10^{18} of water for phenyl ethanol, and about 1 in 3×10^{14} for ionone. He concluded that the eel is in the same class as the dog when it comes to sensitivity.

These threshold concentrations are those at which the smell sensation just begins to be felt. As the concentration is raised above the threshold value the intensity of the sensation naturally gets stronger, but it is hard to give a quantitative account of it because there is no easy way to measure the strength of our feelings and sensations. Nevertheless, there is a generalization or law that tells what happens in a rough sort of way. It is known as the Weber-Fechner Law, and with reservations here and there it applies to physical sensations generally.

For example, you might be shown a collection of paper bags filled with varying amounts of sand, and asked to pick out all those that were the same weight as one standard bag. You must do this by lifting them and can not use a balance or scales. If you weigh the bags after you have made your selection by hand, you will find that your judgment is not pinpoint accurate. Perhaps if the standard weighed 16 ounces, you might find that the ones you picked as being the same weighed anywhere from 15 to 17 ounces. In that case you could say that when the weight was 16 oz., the just noticeable difference in weight ('J.N.D.') is 1 oz., and their ratio is 1/16. If you then repeat the experiment using a standard bag weighing 16 pounds instead of 16 ounces, you will find that you must add or subtract 1 pound to get a J.N.D., and the ratio is again 1/16. If you were to make the standard weigh 32 lb. instead of 16, it would take 2 lb. to make a J.N.D.

46

In the same way, if you were standing in the dark outside a house and looking at two windows, one lit by 1000 candles and the other lit by some other number, you could find out how many candles must be added or subtracted to give a J.N.D. Suppose that the required number was 80 candles, then if the number in the standard room was 100 instead of 1000, the number to give a J.N.D. would be about 8 instead of 80.

The same rule holds with sound intensities, taste sensations, and many other sensory phenomena. Stated generally, if x is the strength of the stimulus as measured in some convenient way (pounds, or candles, or parts per million), and if Δx is the amount by which x must be increased to give a J.N.D., then:

$$\frac{\Delta x}{x} = \text{a constant}$$

This generalization was put forward by Weber more than 100 years ago. Fechner, who is often called the founder of psychophysics, developed it in the following way. If $\Delta x/x = $ constant for the J.N.D., it should be true also for other increments in the stimulus, which is expressed mathematically by writing,

$$dS = C\frac{dx}{x}$$

where dS is an increment in the sensation generated by an increment in the stimulus, dx, superimposed on an already existing stimulus, x, and C is a proportionality constant.

Mathematics is quantitative logic, and once we have expressed an idea in quantitative, mathematical form, the ordinary operations of mathematics allow us to develop the logical, quantitative consequences of our idea. Without going into details, it follows that if,

$$dS = C\frac{dx}{x}$$

then,

$$S = a \log x - a \log x_0$$

where S is the strength of the sensation (measured in some way), $\log x$ is the logarithm of the stimulus that produces the sensation, S, $\log x_0$ is the logarithm of the stimulus that produces a just perceptible (threshold) sensation, and a is a constant.

This logarithmic relation between the strength of the stimulus and the strength of the sensation is called the Weber-Fechner (or Fechner-Weber) Law, and the point of it is that it shows another kind of experiment we can do. (The first kind is simply to show that $\Delta x/x$ = constant for the J.N.D.) If the formula is correct, then a graph in which the sensation, S, is plotted against the logarithm of the stimulus, x, should be a straight line.

Before we see how this test has been applied to smells, there is another point that the formula illustrates. When the concentration of smelly material is zero the smell sensation is naturally zero also. As the concentration builds up from zero, there is no sensation until the concentration reaches and passes the threshold concentration (x_0). The intensity of the sensation and the concentration of the odourous material are therefore distinct because one can be zero even though the other is not.

Scientists at the U.S. Bureau of Mines some years ago used a rough-and-ready method of assigning a number to represent the strength of a smell. They were interested in the possibility of sending a danger-warning signal to men in coal mines by adding a powerful smell to the ventilation system or to the compressed air supply supplied to the pneumatic drills. If this was to work, they had to know how much of the chemical odourant would give a certain strength of smell.

They first built an apparatus for mixing a substance, ethyl mercaptan, which has a powerful and rather unpleasant smell with air in precisely known amounts. Then they got a jury of six observers to smell the various mixtures and to try to estimate the strength of the smell numerically on a 0 to 5 scale, like this:

'0 or no odour requires no amplification; degree 1 is the threshold odour, the just perceptible odour. Consider now the opposite end of the scale; degree 5 or very strong is a most intense odour; it must be perceived, however, only as an odour and aside from any other physiological effects caused by the chemical, such as irritation, nausea, or otherwise; degree 3 or easily noticeable is the medium odour midway in intensity between degrees 1 and 5; degree 2 or faint is conceived as midway between degrees 1 and 3; similarly degree 4 or strong is conceived as midway between degrees 3 and 5. With this scale of 0 and 5 equal degrees the observers recorded their impressions of the odour intensities. They did not always agree closely, but it was found that by employing a number of observers (six generally) and taking averages of the results of their observations, very satisfactory measurements of the odour intensities could be taken.'

One of their observers was not very discriminating (he gave nearly all the smells the same value, 2) and as he was used in less than half the experiments, I have re-plotted their results leaving him out, to make the accompanying graph. Each circle represents the average of 5 (or occasionally 4) separate estimates of the smell strength. The last circle on the left, for example, shows that one person out of five just perceived the smell, giving an average strength of 0·20. The next circle shows a strength of 0·60 because 3 out of 5 could just perceive it.

There are several interesting things about this graph. For one, despite their very rough-and-ready method of 'numbering' the smell

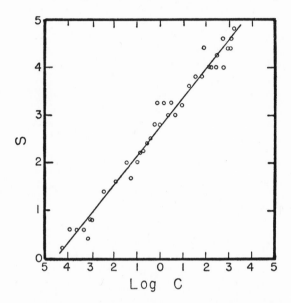

This graph shows the results of Fieldner's experiments with ethyl mercaptan. S is the strength of the smell, estimated on a 0 to 5 scale of intensity; and log C is the logarithm of the number of parts per million of odourant in the air. This is the Weber-Fechner plot. The logarithmic plot of the concentration produces a great expansion at the small end and a great compression of the scale at the large end of the horizontal scale. The range from log $C = -5$ to log $C = 5$ corresponds to a range of concencentrations from 0·00001 to 100,000 parts per million.

sensations, the straight-line relation called for by the Weber-Fechner Law is surprisingly well shown. For another, the spread between the concentration of the weakest and the strongest smells is enormous. If we take the threshold concentration for the average person as somewhere about 1×10^{-3} parts per million of air, the concentration that gave a sensation just short of pain (strength 5) was about 10^4 parts per million, which is ten million times greater than the threshold concentration.

Not only can our noses respond to an enormous number of different smells, but it now appears that their concentration can vary over an enormous range. It follows, though, that we are not as good at perceiving small differences in the strength of a smell as we are at perceiving small differences in its quality. The graph shows, for example, that the concentration of ethyl mercaptan had usually to change by a factor of about 3 to give a just noticeable difference in the smell strength, that is,

$$\frac{\Delta x}{x} = \frac{1}{3} \text{ for 1 J.N.D.}$$

Put in still another way, it means that there are only about 25 or 30 J.N.D.'s between the faintest possible and the strongest possible smell. Our noses are rather poor instruments for quantitative work, but for qualitative work they are superb if they are treated with respect. It also means that in experimenting with smells it is a mistake to try for too much quantitative precision.

This can be important when practical problems come up with such matters as air pollution by industries that generate offensive smells. If we ask members of the public to describe the strength of a smell, we must try not to make very fine distinctions. We must choose our words carefully if we are to avoid unnecessary arguments. For example, if we take the following as a standard terminology and rating scale we will generally find that people seldom differ by more than one unit in their rating:

Rating number	Description
0	No smell
1	Just barely perceptible
2	Distinct
3	Moderate
4	Strong
5	Overpowering

This scale has nothing to do with whether the smell is pleasant or unpleasant. It refers only to the smell strength. The words are carefully chosen to avoid indefinite comparatives like 'very weak' or 'fairly strong'.

Closely connected with all this is one of the most curious of all the many curious things about smell: there are almost no 'character- 'less' smells. Each is distinct, and what is most remarkable, each retains its distinctness pretty well down to the threshold value. Right at the threshold there is usually some indefiniteness, leading to remarks like, '. . . well, I can smell something—but I'm not sure what . . .', but as soon as the strength is increased even very slightly, the response changes to a positive, '. . . there it is—it's faint but I can recognize it . . .'

Our eyes do not have this ability to recognize colours at low levels of illumination. The threshold for colour perception is far above the threshold for just perceiving light in general. This has been traced to the fact that there are two kinds of light-sensitive devices (known as rods and cones) in the retinas of our eyes. The fact that our noses continue to discriminate even at low concentrations may tell us something significant about how they work.

There are many smells that change their character with dilution. Perhaps the best example is the smell of a skunk which is universally abhorred when strong, but which somewhat resembles musk when it is highly diluted and then is disliked mainly for its associations. (Why, otherwise, is musk an almost indispensable ingredient of most highly regarded perfumes, and one of the commonly used scents in toilet soap?) The change of quality with intensity is not the same as the loss of all quality. When our eyes can see light, but not say what colour it is, there has been a loss of quality. For there to be a change of optical quality with intensity, a light that was red at one intensity would have to appear yellow or blue at another, and this does not happen.

The change of odour quality with strength is probably due to the fact that the odour in question is a compound one, made up of several odours which have different thresholds. As the concentration is reduced, the separate components of the odour drop out one by one. What is left still has character, but not the same character.

In recent years, the Weber-Fechner Law has been questioned mainly by S. S. Stevens and his followers in the United States.

For various reasons, Stevens believes that the best way to attach a number to a sensation is to assign a definite value to one sensation and then ask the observers to say whether some other sensation is one-half or one-third, or some other fraction of it, or whether it is 2 or 3 or some other number of times greater than the standard. (Plateau did something like this long ago when he asked eight artists to paint him a grey that was half-way between black and white.) This is different from what Fieldner did: he asked his observers to set up in their minds a sort of linear scale—like a foot rule—and to decide whereabouts on it they thought the smell should come.

One advantage of Stevens' 'ratio estimation' method is that the uncertainty in the ratio can be compared with the size of the ratio, just as the just noticeable change in the stimulus can be related to the size of the stimulus.

To see what this means, let us first go back to the Weber-Fechner relation. There we work with what is essentially a fixed sensation and vary the stimulus, x, to find out how much variation, Δx, it takes to make a just noticeable difference. With Stevens' method of ratio estimation we can do the opposite: we can present two stimuli in a fixed ratio and look to see how much the individual estimates vary. Then, just as Weber compared Δx with x, so Stevens compares ΔS with S.

Because two different shades of grey, for example, retain the same relative brightness in a dim light as in a bright one, Stevens puts,

$$\frac{\Delta S}{S} = n \frac{\Delta x}{x}$$

where S is the sensation measured by the method of ratio estimation, and x is the stimulus measured in some physical units such as pounds or parts per million, and n is a constant of proportionality.

The ordinary operations of mathematics applied to this formula show that,

$$S = \left(\frac{x}{x_0}\right)^n$$

or, alternatively, that,

$$\log S = n \log x - n \log x_0$$

where x_0 is the threshold stimulus.

Once again, the point of this mathematical transformation is that it tells us how to do an experiment. If we measure S by the method of ratio estimation, and plot $\log S$ against $\log x$, we should get a straight line. This has been done, by F. N. Jones, for example, who prepared a series of solutions of benzene in odourless mineral oil and assigned a strength of 10 to the middle solution of the series. He then asked thirty-six observers to rate all the solutions in comparison with this standard and got quite good, reproducible averages; and when the results were plotted in the proper way they gave a fairly good straight line. He did the same thing with several other odourous substances, but unfortunately none of them had very low thresholds so he could not cover the million-fold range of concentrations that Fieldner did.

The difference between the Weber-Fechner plot and the Stevens plot is that in the first one plots S against $\log x$, and in the second,

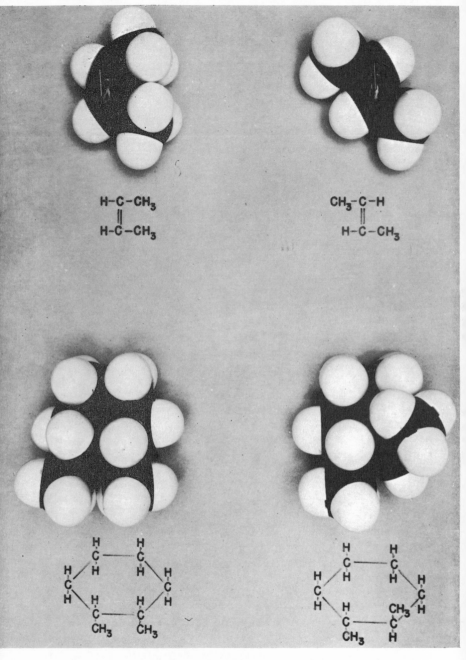

Cis-Trans Isomerism

These models show the isomeric *cis-* and *trans-* forms of 2-butene and of 1,2-dimethyl cyclohexane. These isomers owe their existence to structural rigidities imposed by a double bond and a ring structure respectively. In comparison with the models, the structural formulae are only very roughly pictorial, but they give a much better idea of the way the molecule is put together. This is why structural formulae are more like schematic 'wiring diagrams' than pictures.

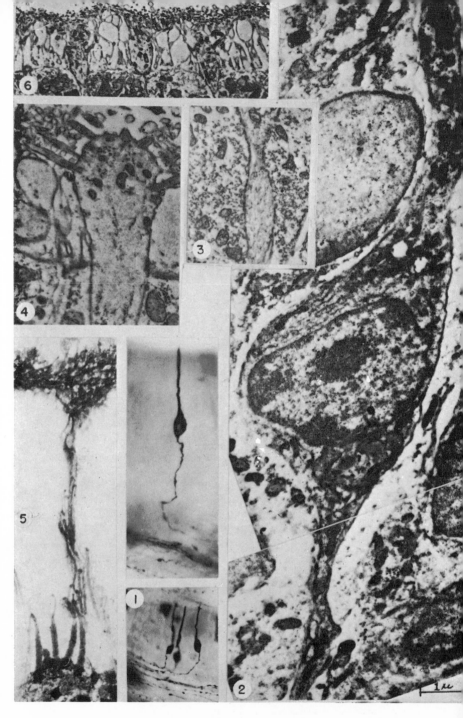

Electron Microscope Photographs of Olfactory Tissues
(*For details, see page 56*)

log S against log x. That these are not the same can be seen if we take Fieldner's data for ethyl mercaptan (which gives a very good straight line by the Weber plot) and re-plot it according to the Stevens method. The graph is distinctly curved, which shows that the two methods of plotting are in fact different. The curvature of the Fieldner data in the Stevens plot does not prove that the Stevens

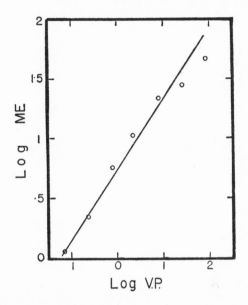

This is the 'Stevens plot' of Jones' results with benzene. The observers were asked to make 'Magnitude Estimates' (M.E.'s) of the smell strength of solutions of benzene by comparing them with a duplicate of the middle solution of the series which was rated as 10. The plot of log M.E. against the Logarithm of the vapour pressure of benzene is approximately straight.

formula is wrong, because Fieldner's subjects were *not* asked to make *ratio estimates* of the smell strength. (This shows how careful one must be in asking questions in psychological experiments— and, for that matter, in all experiments.)

All this probably looks like a finely spun fabric of split hairs, but we will see in later chapters that Stevens' way of measuring sensations

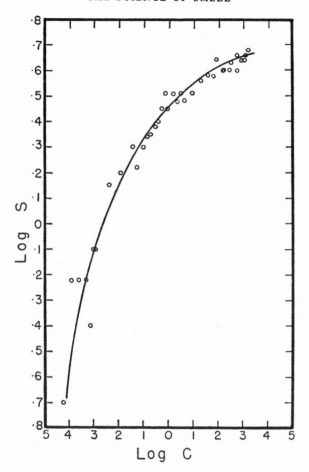

This is the 'Stevens plot' of Fieldner's results with ethyl mercaptan. The line is curved because the observers were asked to estimate the smell intensity, S, on a 0 to 5 scale and not in relation to one standard smell strength.

suggests certain experiments we might not otherwise think of doing, and it may also fit in a little better when we come to think of smells as information.

54

REFERENCES

B. G. BANG. 'Anatomical Evidence for Olfactory Function in Some Species of Birds', *Nature*, **188**, 547–549, 1960.

C. A. ELSBERG, I. LEVY, and E. D. BREWER. 'New Method for Testing the Sense of Smell for Establishment of Olfactory Values of Odourous Substances', *Science*, **83**, 211–212, 1936.

A. C. FIELDNER, R. R. SAYERS, W. P. YANT, S. H. KATZ, J. B. SHOHAN, and R. D. LEITCH. 'Warning Agents for Fuel Gases', U.S. Bureau of Mines, Monograph No. 4, 1931.

E. A. McC. GAMBLE. 'The Applicability of Weber's Law to Smell', *Am. J. Psychol.*, **10**, 82–142, 1898.

W. G. GOFF. 'Measurement of Absolute Olfactory Sensitivity in Rats', *Am. J. Psychol.*, **74**, 384–392, 1961.

A. D. HASLER and W. J. WISBY. 'Repelling Fish by Treatment with Potassium Phenylacetate', U.S. Patent 2,880,133, March 31, 1959.

F. N. JONES. 'Scales of Subjective Intensity for Odours of Diverse Chemical Nature', *Am. J. Psychol.*, **71**, 305–310, 1958.

F. N. JONES. 'Subjective Scales of Intensity for the Three Odours', *Am. J. Psychol.*, **71**, 423–425, 1958.

W. LINDEMANN. (Psychology of the Hedghog.) *Z. Tierpsychol.*, **8**, 224–251, 1951.

W. J. MICHELSEN. 'Procedure for Studying Olfactory Discrimination in Pigeons', *Science*, **130**, 630–631, 1959.

W. NEUHAUS. (Odour Thresholds of Dogs for Ionone and Methyl Mercaptan and their Relation to Other Odour Thresholds of Dog and Man.) *Z. Naturforsch.*, **9b**, 560–567, 1954.

W. NEUHAUS. (Differences in the Acuteness of Olfaction in Dogs.) *Z. vergl. Physiol.*, **40**, 65–72, 1957.

O. T. OWRE and P. O. NORTHINGTON. 'Indication of the Sense of Smell in the Turkey Vulture, *Cathartes aura* (L), from Feeding Tests', *Am. Midland Nat.*, **66**, 200–205, 1961.

W. VAN RIPER. 'Does a Hummingbird Find Its Way to Nectar Through a Sense of Smell?', *Sci. American*, **202**, 157–166, 1960.

E. V. SKRAMLIK. (The Minimum Concentrations Necessary to Arouse Sensations of Smell and Taste.) *Arch. ges. Physiol.* (Pflügers), **249**, 702–716, 1948.

D. M. STEVENS. 'Studies in the Shoaling Behavior of Fish. I. Responses of Two Species to Changes in Illumination and to Olfactory Stimuli', *J. Exptl. Biology*, **36**, 261–280, 1959.

S. S. STEVENS. 'The Psychophysics of Sensory Function', in *Sensory Communication, A Symposium*. W. A. Rosenblith, Editor. M.I.T. Press, Wiley, New York, 1961. pp. 1–33.

H. TEICHMANN. (Concerning the Power of the Olfactory Sense of the Eel. *Anguilla anguilla* (L).) *Z. vergl. Physiol.*, **42**, 206–254, 1959.

H. DeVries and M. Stuiver. 'The Absolute Sensitivity of the Human Sense of Smell', in *Sensory Communication, A Symposium*. W. A. Rosenblith, Editor. M.I.T. Press, Wiley, New York, 1961. pp. 159–167.

B. M. Wenzel. 'Techniques in Olfactometry: A Critical Review of the Last One Hundred Years', *Psychol. Bull.*, **45**, 231–247, 1948.

B. M. Wenzel. 'Olfactometric Method Utilizing Natural Breathing in an Odour-Free "Environment",' *Science*, **121**, 802–803, 1955.

Electron Microscope Photographs of Olfactory Tissues

Illustration facing page 53

1. Two microphotographs of bipolar olfactory cells of a 5-day-old mouse. The axon which leads to the olfactory bulb in the brain is at the bottom. 2. Mounting prepared from three negatives of the olfactory tissues of a rat. It was the only section which chanced to pass through the cell body so as to include also the adjoining parts of the axon (below) and the dendrite (above). Parts of three supporting cells are also included in the picture. 3. Part of the dendrite of a cat. 4. The head of a dendrite, or olfactory vesicle, of a pig. The bases of the cilia or olfactory hairs can be seen, and several are visible in cross-section at the upper left. 5. Cilia rising from the dendrite of a pig, branching and turning off sideways to form the mat of exposed nerve fibres which is the sensory surface on which the odourous molecules impinge. 6. A cross-section of the olfactory epithelium of the pig, showing the heads of three dendrites protruding slightly above the supporting cells. At the top is the felt of olfactory hairs. *Photographs by H. S. Gasser and G. E. Palade, reproduced through the kindness of the Rockefeller Institute and the "Journal of General Physiology".*

8

Smells and Fish

IN April, 1958, some thousands of steelhead fingerlings (*Salmo gairdnerii*) 6 to 8 inches long were released from the Alsea River fish hatchery on the coast of Oregon, U.S.A. Before they were let go they were marked by clipping certain non-essential fins in a peculiar way. Five months later, on September 5, 1958, one of these fish was caught in a net off the coast of Alaska, 2000 miles away. It was then about 14 inches long. It was marked with a numbered tag and put back into the sea. Seventeen months later, on February 5, 1960, this much travelled fish, now more than 2 feet long, turned up at the Alsea hatchery where it had been born two years before.

Some years earlier a similar experiment was carried out on the other side of North America. In 1938, A. G. Huntsman marked 31,359 young Atlantic salmon (*Salmo salar*) before releasing them in the Northeast Margaree River of Cape Breton Island, Nova Scotia. On June 17, 1940, one of these fish was caught, tagged, and released off Bonavista, Newfoundland, and three months later, on September 21, 1940, it was caught by an angler on the Margaree River within two miles of the original release point, and 570 miles by the shortest sea route from Bonavista.

It has long been known that the Atlantic salmon (*Salmo salar*), the steelhead (*Salmo gairdnerii*), and the various species of Pacific salmon (*Oncorhyncus kisutch*, *O. nerka*, etc.) which spawn in fresh water streams, migrate to the sea for several years (two to seven depending on the species) before returning to their home stream to lay their eggs. What was unique about these experiments was the fact that these particular fish were registered and marked before they left the home stream, re-registered and re-marked far out in the ocean, and registered a third time when they came home. Until that had been done it could not be known for sure that the fish that returned had ever gone beyond the estuary of their home stream during their life at sea.

Other fish have been tagged on the high seas and later recaptured during their spawning run into a stream a thousand or more miles from where they were tagged. In these cases it could not be known for sure that the fish were *returning*, but it was rendered overwhelmingly

57

probable by experiments such as one in which 469,326 Pacific salmon fingerlings (*O. nerka*) were marked before leaving a spawning ground at Cultus Lake, British Columbia, on a tributary of the Fraser River. In due course, 16,553 of them were recovered as adults, 4,995 actually in Cultus Lake and 11,558 in the approaches to it, and although traps were placed in nearby tributaries of the Fraser, practically none of the marked fish strayed into them.

Not all the experiments have given results as precise as this. There is usually some straying, and indeed both the homing of the majority and the straying of the minority are necessary to ensure the biological survival of the species.

In an earlier chapter, I explained the biological advantage to an insect that chooses an egg-laying site with precision. Exactly the same reasoning applies here. If a fish has grown to maturity and is ready to spawn, it must have survived all the hazards of an uncertain and dangerous world. The first step to success took place when it was born in what proved to be a favourable environment, and so, if it can lay its eggs in identically the same environment, it may not be the best possible, but it will be one that was demonstrably favourable. At the same time, some straying is desirable if new 'fish runs' are ever to be established in new streams. This may be necessary if the way to the original home is blocked by a landslide or an artificial obstruction like a power dam. A new run can be established only if a few fish are willing to try something new.

On the west coast of North America, each stream, and often each tributary may have its own 'run' of salmon, which can be predicted with some precision. On occasion when a run has been lost as a result of some geological or hydrological calamity, a new and previously unknown run has later been found somewhere else and presumed to represent a transfer from the lost run.

There is an important hint here that has been followed up and verified.

The 'homing' of the fish is not an inherited (that is, a genetically determined) preference for a certain locality. If it were, the offspring of 'strayed' fish would still go back to the ancestral stream and no new runs could be established.

Normally, the place where the eggs are laid is the same as the place where they are hatched, but the two places do not have to be the same, and it is interesting to see what happens when they are switched in a scientific experiment. For example, in 1949 a large number of eggs of the sockeye salmon (*O. nerka*) were collected on the spawning grounds of the Horsefly River in British Columbia, and transported in tanks to a fish hatchery on Horsefly Lake where they were allowed

The rivers and streams shown on this map of British Columbia are the ones that support salmon runs. Streams in the north-east corner of the Province drain into the Arctic Ocean; and streams in the south-east corner that used to provide spawning grounds have been cut off from the sea by hydroelectric dams in the United States. The north-west corner is mostly unexplored.

to hatch and where they spent their first year. There is a range of mountains between the Horsefly River and Horsefly Lake so the eggs were spawned in one water-shed area and hatched in an entirely different one. In 1950, 94,000 fingerlings from these eggs were taken by air to the mouth of the Horsefly River, where it empties into Quesnel Lake, and released there after 64,500 of them had been marked. From there they made their way to the sea in the normal way.

In 1952 when some of them were due to return as three-year olds, a close watch was kept for them at the Horsefly River spawning grounds and also at the hatchery on Horsefly Lake. At the spawning ground, 6829, three-year old sockeye were counted and 2228 were examined for the hatchery mark. None was marked. On the other hand, at the hatchery thirteen three-year old sockeye turned up, nine of them marked, and this at a place where no sockeye had previously been taken.

Since not all sockeye return after three years, the watch was continued into 1953. On the Horsefly River, 105,000 four-year old fish were counted and 46,917 were checked for the hatchery mark. Only one had it. Meanwhile at the hatchery, 203 marked and 66 unmarked sockeye were taken actually at the end of the outlet pipe, and 15 more marked fish were found which had spawned and died downstream from the hatchery.

The time of this new run to the hatchery coincided with the regular run to the Horsefly River, showing that the timing of the run is probably inherited but its destination can be changed.

This experiment (and similar experiments elsewhere) showed that the fish did not return to the stream their parents preferred, but to the one in which they themselves were hatched and spent their 'impressionable years'. Thus the homing is not a genetic character but is the result of what is called 'imprinting'. This is the name given to a now well-recognized phenomenon in which animals, birds, or fish become endowed with a lifelong trait or behaviour pattern as a result of being exposed to (or 'imprinted' with) a certain environmental factor at a certain critical period which is usually rather early in their development.

The experiment just described is only one of several which show that the home stream migration of salmon is a result of imprinting rather than a matter of some mysterious 'homing instinct', but it has an added feature of profound significance. The eggs that were laid on the Horsefly River were transported by air over the mountains to the hatchery, and the fingerlings were later flown from the hatchery to the release point on Quesnel Lake. Therefore, when these fish came back as part of the regular Horsefly River run, and had the choice of going either to the hatchery or the spawning ground, which-ever destination they chose had to be reached by way of a route they had never before travelled. Their success in reaching the hatchery was therefore not due to any memory of a trip downstream four years earlier, and they actually had to turn aside and leave their companions of the regular run. What they 'remembered' then was not the topography but the smell of their foster home stream, and this 'memory' took them right to the effluent pipe of the hatchery.

That they really did smell their way home was shown by the follow-ing experiment.

In the State of Washington, U.S.A., there is a small stream called the Issaquah, which supports a very convenient run of coho salmon (*Oncorhyncus kisutch*). At one point the stream divides with a small tributary called the East Fork leading off from the main stream. Both branches support runs to separate spawning grounds. In November, 1952, A. D. Hasler and W. J. Wisby established a fish trap on the East Fork about a mile and a half above the junction. There was already a trap on the main stream a mile up from the fork. The procedure was to capture fish which had followed either the main stream or the East Fork, mark them with tags, and trans-port them back to a place below the fork. Before releasing them, some had their olfactory organs plugged with vaseline, or benzocaine ointment, or cotton, or in some cases a combination of these, while others were returned to the water with their smelling apparatus intact.

Altogether, 302 fish were moved back down stream, 226 from the main Issaquah and 76 from the East Fork. Of the 302, 153 had their olfactory pits plugged before they were released, and 149 were left unplugged as controls. Not all these fish were recaptured, but those that were told a very consistent story. Of the controls from the main Issaquah, 46 were recaptured and all were found in the Issaquah which was their original choice. Of the controls from the East Fork, 27 were recaptured, 19 back again in the East Fork and 8 in the main Issaquah. The ability of these fish to repeat their first choice was not perfect, but it was remarkably good.

The fish whose noses were stopped up distributed themselves in an essentially random way between the two streams, if we allow for the fact that the main Issaquah is much larger than the East Fork. The original catch was 226 from the Issaquah and 76 from the East Fork: a ratio of 3 to 1 approximately. Fifty-one plugged fish originally from the Isaaquah were recaptured, 39 there and 12 in the East Fork, again a ratio of 3 to 1 very nearly. Nineteen East Fork fish with plugs were recaptured, 16 in the main stream and 3 in the fork, for a

61

ratio of 5 to 1 which, considering the small numbers, is not significantly different from the previous ratio of 3 to 1.

It is strange in view of the importance of the whole matter, that this experiment which was performed as recently as 1952, was almost the first that was designed to show that the homing behaviour of salmon has a material, olfactory basis and does not depend on anything so intangible as a 'homing instinct' or as esoteric as extra-sensory perception. Hasler and Wisby had previously (in 1951) reported a pilot experiment on the discrimination of stream odours by fishes, but apart from that only one other worker (E. H. Craigie in 1925) had seriously tried to show by experiment that the migration of sockeye salmon used smell as a guide-post.

REFERENCES

E. H. CRAIGIE. 'A Preliminary Experiment on the Relation of the Olfactory Sense to the Migration of Sockeye Salmon', *Trans. Roy. Soc. Canada*, (V), Ser. 3, **20**, 215–224, 1926.

R. E. FOERSTER. 'The Return from the Sea of Sockeye Salmon, with Special Reference to Percentage Survival, Sex Proportions and Progress of Migration', *J. Biol. Board, Can.*, **3** (1), 26–42, 1936.

A. D. HASLER and W. J. WISBY. 'Discrimination of Stream Odours by Fishes and its Relation to Parent Stream Behavior', *Amer. Naturalist*, **85**, 223–238, 1951.

A. D. HASLER. 'Guideposts of Migrating Fishes', *Science*, **132**, 785–92, 1960.

A. G. HUNTSMAN. 'Return of Marked Salmon from a Distant Place', *Science*, **95**, 381–382, 1942.

INTERNATIONAL PACIFIC SALMON FISHERIES COMMISSION. 'Annual Report, 1953', pp. 22–30.

W. J. WISBY and A. D. HASLER. 'Effect of Olfactory Occlusion on Migrating Silver Salmon', *J. Fisheries Res. Bd. Can.*, **11**, 472–478, 1954.

9

Homing by Fish

THE Fraser River system in British Columbia embraces a very large complex of salmon spawning grounds. The total discharge from the river at its mouth varies from a mid-winter low of about 50,000 cubic feet per second to a high of over 500,000 during the early summer freshet. If the discharge during a typical salmon run is taken as about 200,000 cu. ft. per sec., it may well be asked how it is possible for the characteristic local smell of a small spawning ground —such as the discharge from the hatchery on Horsefly Lake—to be recognized in this enormous volume of water when it passes into the sea.

The Weber-Fechner Law provides at least part of the answer.

If you will refer back to the graph showing how the smell of ethyl mercaptan varied with concentration, you will see, for example, that to reduce the intensity from degree 3 (moderate) to degree 1 (threshold) requires something like a 5000-fold dilution. If the total river discharge is 200,000 cu. ft. per sec., an input of only 40 cu. ft. per sec. will be diluted by a factor of 5000 when it reaches the mouth, because 40 × 5000 = 200,000. Thus a comparatively modest addition of water with only a moderate concentration of the home stream scent in it can put its mark on the whole down stream system. Note, too, that the figures given above are merely by way of example. If the home stream scent was at strength 4 at the source, dilution to threshold would call for about 100,000 volumes of water, and if the main river discharge was down to 100,000 cu. ft. per second, the flow of the home stream would need to be no more than one cubic foot per second, or 375 gallons per minute—which is less than that from a good-sized fire hose.

The ability of the fish to move from the mouth of the river up to a pre-determined small destination, such as the discharge pipe from the Horsefly River hatchery, is wonderful and astonishing, and infinitely interesting, but it is not magic. It is exactly on a par with the ability of a male moth to locate a female from a mile away, or of a dog to follow its master's scent along a well-travelled street.

We are still a long way from knowing what kind of chemical molecules give the home stream its characteristic smell, and we still don't know the sequence of responses by which the fish homes in on the source. They may not be as blindly mechanical as the responses of the fruit fly described in Chapter 4, but fish behaviour is likely to have more in common with the insect's than with a man's. We must not make the mistake of crediting the fish with our kind of intelligence. For example, migrating salmon that have already turned aside into a minor tributary have been caught and tagged, and then put back into the main stream *above* their proper turn-off. These fish have later been re-captured a second time back in their home stream, showing that when they missed its scent they must have turned back and swum down stream, actually going the opposite way to masses of other fish *en route* to other spawning grounds higher up the river. It would be easy to think of this as showing a highly developed intelligence, and the fish may actually be highly intelligent, but their behaviour does not prove that they are. After all, their back-tracking to regain the scent is exactly what our fruit flies did when they lost the scent from the fermenting banana.

The chemical make-up of the attractive scent is still unknown. It is definitely not anything as simple as water temperature or something like the salt content or a difference in carbon dioxide concentration—all of which have been suggested at one time or another. Hasler and Wisby in their pilot studies preceding the Issaquah Creek experiments, made some small-scale laboratory trials at the University of Wisconsin using bluntnose minnows (*Hyborhynchus notatus*) as test animals. They first picked out two local streams that passed through different geological formations and collected water in plastic bags from each. The water was frozen and stored in a deep freeze until needed. Back in the laboratory, they set up two aquariums with an arrangement for feeding water from the two creeks into opposite ends of each aquarium. The minnows in one aquarium were then trained to associate the smell of one stream with their 'dinner time' and the smell of the other with an electric shock; and the minnows in the other aquarium were given the same training but with the streams reversed.

The results were very satisfactory.

The minnows could be taught quite definitely to recognize the smell of each stream and give the correct response depending on whether they had been trained to associate it with food or a shock. When their olfactory organs were surgically or otherwise destroyed they lost this ability even though their behaviour was otherwise normal. This proved that they really were recognizing the smell of the streams.

When the water was boiled away leaving only the mineral residue behind, and this residue was re-dissolved in distilled water, they no longer recognized it. Therefore the smell was not in the mineral matter. Also, when the water was simply boiled the smell was lost. This could mean that the smell was destroyed by heat, or that it was driven off with the steam. When the steam was collected and condensed the fish did not recognize the condensate, so that the compounds giving rise to the smell were clearly sensitive to heat. When the water was carefully distilled in a vacuum so that the temperature never rose above that of the room, the minnows recognized the distillate but not the residue, showing that the smell-substance was volatile. That was as far as the experiments were taken except for one additional and highly important observation.

The minnows were trained to recognize water collected during the summer. When they were tested with water taken from the two streams during the winter they recognized it as well as ever. The winter climate of Wisconsin is cold enough to freeze the surface of the ground and reduce the run-off to a minimum, and of course the vegetation is nearly all dormant. The constancy of the stream odour under these conditions has an enormous significance both theoretically and practically from its relation to the constancy of the salmon migrations.

Scientists of the Fisheries Research Board of Canada are currently extending this work on home stream odours, to see whether adult sockeye salmon in a tank will respond in a recognizable way when water from their own home stream is added to the tank. Using full-grown salmon instead of minnows puts the whole project on a rather heroic scale, but at least the fish don't have to be trained. The experiments are still going on, and so far they have shown that the salmon do react visibly to water from their own home stream, and that the odour is due to some substance or combination of substances in the water that can be destroyed by heat and is neither acid nor alkaline.

It will probably take a long time to run down and identify the odourous substances by these experiments because it needs so little of them to produce an effect. A side line to this work will make this clear.

It has long been a matter of common knowledge to the biologists studying salmon migration that a run of fish up a fish ladder or through a narrow place in the stream can be temporarily stopped by dipping one's hand in the water, or even by spitting into it. The paw of an animal such as a bear, or a bit of sea lion skin dipped in the water will have the same effect. Clearly this is a type of alarm reaction that has considerable survival value to a species that is preyed upon by various wild animals during its spawning run upstream. (It is interesting that young fish on their way *downstream* to the sea do not show the reaction.) When the existence of a substance producing this alarm reaction was recognized, it was given the name of 'mammalian skin factor'. Unlike the home stream odour, the source of the skin factor was known and it could be procured at will (though in unimaginably small amounts) simply by soaking one's hands in a litre of water for a minute or two.

By chemically fractionating these extracts, and also extracts from bear's paws and sea lion skins, and testing the various fractions in a stream at a time when the fish were running, the active substance (or at least one of them) was identified as an amino acid called 1-serine which is a constituent of proteins and which has the structure,

$$HO—CH_2—CH—COOH$$
$$\mid$$
$$NH_2$$

It can evoke an alarm reaction at concentrations as low as 1 part in 80,000,000,000 of water. Evidently it would have been much more difficult to isolate and identify it if its source had been unknown and if 'concentrated' solutions from hand washings had not been available.

When the direct way to solve a problem seems likely to be tedious or expensive, it is legitimate and sensible to look for an indirect way around the difficulty. In this case, it is hard to identify chemically the true home stream odour because there are so many irrelevant substances in the water along with it. The most generally useful short-cut to a correct answer to an intractable problem is by a device I have called a working hypothesis. That is, we try to guess the correct answer, and then, assuming it to be true, we think through its logical consequences to a prediction of something not already known that can be tested experimentally. (I have already described one such working hypothesis—that was completely but rewardingly wrong— in connection with the mechanism of the up wind guidance of fruit flies.) As an exercise in scientific speculation, I will develop a working hypothesis of the source of the home stream odour and show how it might be tested.

We start with the knowledge that once a salmon has left the sea and entered the river, the guide posts it follows are odourous. The odour is one that remains constant from summer to winter and from year to year, and it is not affected by logging and land-clearing operations, or by changes in farming practices and crops, or by pollution from cities and industries of the most varied sort. There-fore it is unlikely that the home stream odour originates in the soil or vegetation of the water-shed area. Therefore it is most likely to originate in the water itself, that is, in the water weeds or the resident population of non-migratory fishes.

At first sight the water plants would look to be the most probable source of the odour because they are usually rooted to the stream bed. However, they can be loosened and moved along by floods or left behind if the stream cuts itself a new channel, so that their immobility and local fixation may be more apparent than real.

The local fish population is seemingly very mobile, but there are signs that it may be more fixed than the plants.

G. E. Gunning at the Indiana University made some very revealing studies in a small stream (Rockland Creek, Indiana) by tagging and moving small fish, the longear sunfish (*Lepomis megalotis*) and showed that they keep to a surprisingly small home range. The precision of their homing reactions was remarkable and it apparently depended on smell because blinded fish got home perfectly well but fish with their smelling organs destroyed did not. The performance of one fish was remarkable. It was first taken on July 10, 1958, in a certain part of the stream where there was a large rock which served as a land-mark. It was blinded and released about 350 feet downstream. On August 11, it was re-taken near the same rock and again moved back downstream. On August 16 it was caught again within 10 feet of the same rock and moved downstream for the third time, and on September 8 it was caught only 3 feet from the rock. It was then taken to the laboratory and its blindness positively verified. (Incidentally, blinding the fish did not handicap them as much as you might think, because the water in the stream is normally very muddy and turbid.)

Evidently then, the local, resident, non-migratory fish population of a stream can be very conservative in its territorial behaviour because its very mobility gives it the means to avoid movement. This kind of thing is just what is needed to build up a local race or family differing in more or less subtle ways from similar families elsewhere. Just as each colony of bees develops its own hive odour, so each local race of resident fish must develop its own home range odour. It may originate in the fish themselves or in some associated organism such as a fungus or bacterium.

So far we are on firm ground provided by experiments like Gunning's and similar work by Hasler and others. We can now make an assumption or working hypothesis that the home stream odour that guides the salmon is the same as the home range odour of one or other of the local, non-migratory fish species.

If this assumption is correct, then we should be able to generate a concentrated home stream odour by collecting representatives of the local, resident fish population of a certain stream and placing them in separate jars of water for a time. We would then observe how adult migrating salmon from that stream, and from other streams, react to the water in the various jars.

If the experiment fails, we will still be a little farther on because we will have eliminated one possibility. If its succeeds, we will be a lot farther on because we will have found a concentrated source of the home stream odour in which to track down the actual chemicals responsible for it.

So far as I know, this suggestion has not been made before and the experiment has still to be tried.

REFERENCES

D. F. ALDERDICE, J. R. BRETT, D. R. IDLER, and U. FAGERLUND. 'Further Observations on Olfactory Perception in Migrating Adult Coho and Spring Salmon—Properties of the Repellent Mammalian Skin', *Fisheries Res. Bd. Can., Prog. Rept. Pac. Coast Stations*, No. 98, 1954.

S. D. GERKING. 'Restricted Movements of Fish Populations', *Biol. Rev.*, **34**, 221–242, 1959.

G. E. GUNNING. 'The Sensory Basis for Homing in the Longear Sunfish', *Invest. Indiana Lakes and Streams*, V, No. 3, 103–130, 1959.

A. D. HASLER and W. J. WISBY. 'Discrimination of Stream Odours by Fishes and its Relation to Parent Stream Behavior', *Amer. Naturalist*, **85**, 223–238, 1951.

A. D. HASLER and W. J. WISBY. 'The Return of Displaced Largemouth Bass and Green Sunfish to a "Home" Area', *Ecology*, **39**, 289–293, 1958.

D. R. IDLER, J. R. MCBRIDE, R. E. E. JONAS, and N. TOMLINSON. 'Olfactory Perception in Migrating Salmon. II. Studies on a Laboratory Bioassay for Homestream Water and Mammalian Repellent', *Can. J. Biochem. Physiol.*, **39**, 1575–84, 1961.

D. R. IDLER, U. H. FAGERLUND, and H. MAYOH. 'Olfactory Perception in Migrating Salmon. I. L-Serine, a Salmon Repellent in Mammalian Skin', *J. Gen. Physiol.*, **39**, 889–892, 1956.

H. KALMUS and C. R. RIBBANDS. 'The Origin of the Odours by which Honeybees Distinguish Their Companions', *Proc. Roy. Soc.*, Ser. B, **140**, 50–59, 1952.

H. KLEEREKOPER and J. A. MORGENSEN. 'The Chemical Composition of the Scent of Fresh Water Fish, With Special Reference to Amines and Amino Acids', *Z. Vergl. Physiol.*, **42**, 492–500, 1959.

W. PFEIFFER. 'The Fright Reaction of Fish', *Biol. Rev.*, **37**, 495–511, 1962.

D. A. RAMSAY and A. D. HASLER. 'Olfactory Cues in Migrating Salmon', *Science*, **133**, 56–57, 1961.

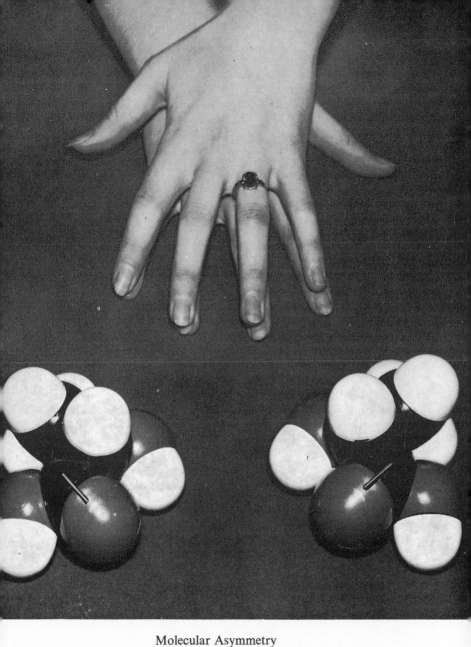

Molecular Asymmetry

Lactic acid, $CH_3-\overset{\overset{\displaystyle H}{|}}{\underset{\underset{\displaystyle OH}{|}}{C}}-\overset{\overset{\displaystyle O}{\|}}{C}-OH$, is one of the simplest substances possessing

an asymmetric carbon atom and showing optical isomerism. The two molecules, like the two hands, are similar but cannot be superimposed.

The Stereochemical Theory of Olfaction

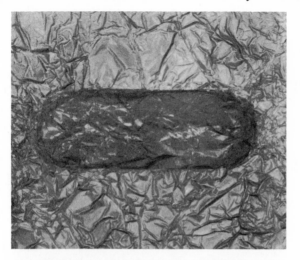

Amoore's 'Ethereal' Site

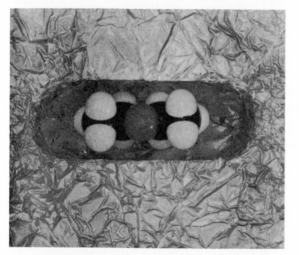

A Molecule of Diethyl Ether in the 'Ethereal' Site

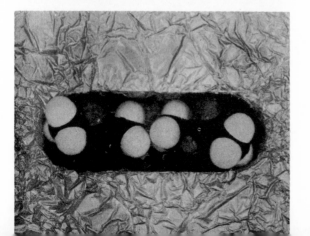

Two Molecules of Methyl Acetate in the 'Ethereal' Site

Amoore's
'Camphoraceous'
Site

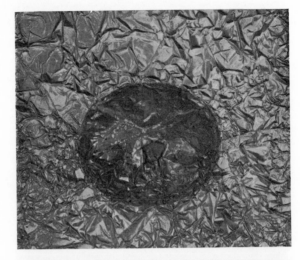

A Cyclo-Octane
Molecule in the
'Camphoraceous'
Site

A Chloretone
Molecule in the
'Camphoraceous'
Site

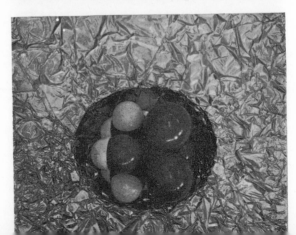

The Stereochemical Theory of Olfaction

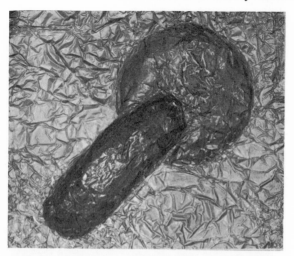

Amoore's 'Floral' Site

A Geraniol Molecule in the 'Floral' Site

A Rosetone Molecule in the 'Floral' Site

T. J. WALKER and A. D. HASLER. 'Detection and Discrimination of Odours of Aquatic Plants by the Bluntnose Minnow', *Physiol. Zool.*, **22**, 45–63, 1949.

POSTSCRIPT TO CHAPTER 9

On the evidence there can be no doubt that salmon smell their way up the home stream to their predetermined spawning ground. Their journey from a distant point in the open ocean to the river's mouth is another matter, and I can think of two lines of evidence to show that the open sea migration is not and cannot be an olfactory response.

The first is simply a matter of arithmetic.

The Fraser River of British Columbia is an unusually big salmon river. If we take its average discharge as two hundred thousand cubic feet per second (and for much of the year it is less than half this) it amounts to substantially less than one cubic mile of water per day. In the immensity of the Pacific Ocean any attractive odour it might contain would soon be diluted far below any conceivable threshold. Other streams have rates of discharge several orders of magnitude smaller and still support regular runs of salmon. Add to this the fact that the migrating fish must regularly traverse water masses of quite different origin and you can only conclude that the fish cannot possibly find their way back to the mouth of their home stream by smell, starting from 500 or 1000 miles offshore.

Even if the smell was there in sufficient quantity, it still could not provide a directional guidance if we recall the experiments on the up-wind movement of the fruit flies described in Chapter 4. Smell is inherently non-directional, and the flies could only fly to the source of the odour when there was a wind blowing. In the open ocean of the North Pacific there are currents with speeds up to about three miles per day. Not only is this much less than the one to two miles per hour wind velocity that gives direction to the insects, but the fish must sometimes swim with the flow, sometimes across it, and sometimes against it to get home.

The problem of deep-sea navigation by fish is as difficult as it is fascinating. It will not be easy or cheap to solve because ships are expensive research tools.

There are some indications that some fish at least do navigate by the sun and stars. European eels which mature in the rivers and then migrate to the mid-Atlantic to spawn in the Sargasso Sea, show an extraordinary eye-development before setting out on their astonishing journey. What is most curious is the fact that, to steer by the sun, they must have some kind of internal, biological 'clock' to allow for the daily, dawn-to-dusk movement of the sun across the sky. This is not as incredible as it may sound, for there is some evidence that bees have and use just such a time-sense in directing their foraging journeys.

REFERENCES

K. VON FRISCH. *Bees, Their Vision, Chemical Senses, and Language.* Cornell University Press, 1950.

A. D. HASLER. 'Perception of Pathways by Fishes in Migration', *Quart. Rev. Biol.*, **31**, 200–209, 1956.

A. D. HASLER, R. HORRALL, W. J. WISBY, and W. BRAEMER. 'Evidence for a Sun-Orientation Mechanism in Fishes', *Limnol. Oceanogr.*, **3**, 353–361, 1958.

A. D. HASLER. 'Guideposts of Migrating Fishes', *Science*, **132**, 785–792, 1960.

S. B. HENDRICKS. 'Metabolic Control of Timing', *Science*, **141**, 21–27, 1963.

10

Dogs

THE first thing a beginner in science has to learn is how hard it is to make an experiment come out right when you know what the result should be. Strangely, though, it takes rather longer to learn that this is also true when you do not know the answer and are depending on the experiment to give it. In Chapter 7, for example, we saw that when people are asked to estimate the strength of a smell, a rather simple change in the way the question is worded will make the answers conform to one or the other of two quite distinct formulae.

When we are asking a dog to do our smelling for us, the problem is especially difficult. The animal is infinitely more intelligent than an insect, and so it does not give a simple, mechanical, unit response to a simple unit stimulus. He is much too subtle for that, but his intelligence is different from ours. He is more distractable, more emotional, more interested in action than contemplation, so that what he seems to be doing and what he really is doing may not be the same thing at all. For example, Most and Brückner arranged to have a man walk half way across a field of rather soft earth, and then caused his trail to vanish into thin air by carrying him away with a trolley attached to an overhead cable. The trail was continued on-wards by a large wheel with shoes fixed at one-pace intervals around the rim. A dog was set to follow the trail, and it continued past the change-over point apparently without noticing any difference. The experimenters concluded that the animal followed the track in virtue of a great variety of odours, and that the smell of newly disturbed earth and bruised vegetation might be as important as the specific odours left by the quarry (which, in the case of a man or woman, could include the odours of leather, shoe polish, soap and even perfume superimposed on the natural odour of the skin). It seems likely, too, that their dog was using his eyes as well as and perhaps even more than his nose, and not only to see the visible disturbance of the ground but also to watch the demeanour of his master. This last can be very important, and in any experiment with an animal it is absolutely essential that the handler should not know the correct answer to the problem the animal is trying to solve.

There was once a circus horse which astonished everyone with its ability to do sums in arithmetic and tap out the answers with its hoof. The performance seemed to be quite uncanny until it was noticed that when its master did not know the answer the horse was likely to tap its way past the correct result. Its master was unconsciously tense until it reached the right figure and then relaxed imperceptibly to everyone but the horse, which took this as the signal to stop tapping. The name of the horse was Clever Hans, and this experimental hazard is sometimes called the 'Clever Hans Error'.

In an attempt to avoid it, Becker, Markee, and King tried to arrange a 'problem box' in which a dog would be trained to solve a problem as far as possible by itself and without a handler. Their paper is an epic of frustration and a textbook example of the operation of 'Murphy's Law' ('Any error that can possibly creep in, will') and its First Corollary: 'When nothing can possibly go wrong, something does'.

Their dogs simply refused to be machines. One does not need to know the details of their experimental method to savour this account of the breaking-in of a new animal: '. . . the first 5–7 trials were always difficult. Naive dogs twisted about in the central chamber, clawed walls, stood on hind legs, or sat and howled. When, by chance, they first approached and sniffed at a cone, a buzzer sounded and the retaining walls of the central chamber rolled back allowing a choice of right or left turn. After 10–15 trials, a dog would ram its nose into the cone and cock its ears in anticipation of the buzzer. If we purposely delayed sounding the buzzer, the dog would withdraw its nose, look at the side walls, and push its nose back into the cone. It was, of course, impossible to tell what the dog's olfactory experience was in such a situation . . .' And again, '. . . the dog very quickly learned what was necessary to gain egress, and escape became its prime motive, not olfactory discrimination. However, when, by chance or design, a dog executed a correct turn it seldom neglected to pick up its meat reward on the way out.'

To avoid this sort of difficulty, it is usually more satisfactory to have a handler with the dog, but he should not know the answer either. Moulton, Ashton, and Eayrs, for example, compared the odour thresholds for the first eight aliphatic acids in an experimental hut, 12 feet square, which was divided into three rooms, one for the supervisor, one for the main experiment, and one for the dog and its handler to occupy while the supervisor was arranging the experiment. While the dog was working, the supervisor sat in his own cubicle, and all communication was by means of signal lights turned on and off by push buttons.

Without going to this amount of elaboration, there are two kinds of experiment that tell us a great deal about the olfactory powers of dogs and a little about olfaction itself. These are retrieving experiments where the dog has to select and bring back an object that has been handled by a designated person, and tracking experiments in which it must follow the trail of one person among several.

Retrieving experiments are easily arranged and are a regular feature of exhibitions of dog training. It is not easy to avoid the 'Clever Hans Error' because of the presence of many onlookers, but it is probably not a serious experimental hazard if the observers keep their distance. Some very significant results have been secured by this method.

Löhner, for example, used carefully cleaned wooden sticks that were baked in an oven to deodourize them and were thereafter handled with tongs. The dog's task was to pick out from some 10 to 20 control sticks the one stick that had been in contact with a designated person. The results showed that, given more than two minutes contact time, the finger tips alone could impart a recognizable odour to the stick, and if it was grasped in the whole hand, a few seconds contact was enough. Prior or subsequent handling by others did not prevent the animal from identifying it correctly. Moreover, although the dog always took the scent from the recently washed hand of the observer, it could successfully identify a stick that had been in contact with some other part of the observer's body. Löhner was careful to avoid the 'Clever Hans Error'.

More recently, Kalmus has repeated and confirmed all these experiments, using freshly laundered and ironed handkerchiefs instead of sticks. The most interesting thing about his experiments was the inclusion of four pairs of identical twins in the group of test subjects.

The experiments showed that the dogs he used had no difficulty in distinguishing between people who were unrelated, or even between members of the same family, provided they were not monozygotic twins. With the twins, they would pick out a handkerchief scented by one after sniffing the hand of the other. If handkerchiefs scented by both twins were laid out along with the controls, the dog invariably brought back the first 'twin' handkerchief it came to.

Thus it appears that the dog recognizes the individual's scent pattern from whatever part of the body it comes, and even though it is over- and under-laid by an alien scent pattern. The scent pattern must be genetically fixed because only identical (monozygotic) twins have the same genetic constitution, and their scents are clearly very similar indeed. The scent cannot depend on diet, clothing, or home environment, because in one of Kalmus' experiments, the twins were men, thirty-three years old, married, and living in different places.

73

Tracking is a much more difficult task for the dog than retrieving, because the accidental odours and the strength of the prime odour will vary tremendously as the trail passes from grassland to asphalt pavement, and from ploughed earth to solid rock. Only a well-trained dog can perform accurately and reliably in these experiments, and the trainer or handler must be careful not to change his customary procedure, because even slight variations can cause complete failure for a whole day. Only a few of the reported investigations fulfill the requirements for really reliable results.

One of the earliest was reported by Romanes as long ago as 1885. In one of his experiments, he lined up twelve men one behind the other with himself in the lead, and they set off with each man treading carefully in the footprints of the man in front. After going about 200 yards in this way, the party split, with Romanes and five men going off to the right and the other six turning to the left. After they had gone a considerable distance they all hid, and Romanes' dog was put on the trail and told to find her master. She did so with only a slight check due to overshooting at the place where the party divided. Romanes took pains to see that the dog had to depend on scent alone, and the dog was, of course, well trained and practiced. It did not make the same mistake as the less well-qualified animal used by Most and Brückner which was as willing to follow the track-laying wheel as the man.

In another experiment, Romanes found that the dog followed him very well when he wore his own boots for part of the trail, and then took them off and continued barefoot. When he wrapped his boots in brown paper, the dog could no longer recognize his trail until the paper became torn, and she was content to follow another man who was wearing Romanes' boots.

All this goes to show that when a dog is genuinely following a scent, it recognizes the actual, physical presence of something left behind on the ground by its quarry. It may gain some additional guidance from disturbed soil or plants, but the primary clue is olfactory. An untrained dog is likely to be guided mainly by the visible trail and will often follow a man as well when he is walking on stilts as when he is on his own feet. The fact that the trail depends on physical contact with the ground is suggested by an experiment of Most and Brückner where they used their overhead cable to carry a man across a field close to the ground but without actually touching it, and found there was nothing for the dog to follow.

The true scent trail is a matter of individual bodily secretions, originating in the feet, and working their way out through the shoes. It is significant that new shoes will not leave an individual trail until

74

they have been worn for a day or two, and rubber overshoes will also suppress the individuality.

In view of all this, it is interesting to see what Kalmus found when he used identical twins in his tracking experiments. As might be expected from the retrieving tests, if the dog was given the scent of one twin it was perfectly willing to follow and accept the other in a tracking experiment where only the second twin was included in the party.

If, however, a group that included *both* twins walked across a field and then fanned out in various directions and hid, the dog could follow the correct twin whose scent it had been given. It seems clear that the identical twins have scents which are very similar indeed, but which are not completely identical. The situation is rather similar to our own visual problem when we meet one of a pair of twins on the street and are not sure which one it is, even though we may be able to tell them apart when we have them both together.

Kalmus mentions that in one of his experiments, a dog that had successfully tracked one of the twins, became confused and agitated when it was unexpectedly confronted with both of them at the same time.

The physical basis of these recognition and tracking phenomena has been investigated in a very thorough way by W. Neuhaus.

He began by designing an apparatus in which exceedingly small but controlled amounts of odourous material could be added to an air stream. (This is not an easy thing to do when the amount to be added is many millions of times smaller than the total air flow, and his method of solving the problem was both simple and precise.) He then arranged three little boxes with hinged lids so that a lump of sugar could be concealed in one of them at the same time that the scented air was released just in front of it. The other two boxes were blanks and the air discharged before them was unscented. A dog was trained to associate the smell with the sugar reward, and to choose the right box by the presence of the smell. It was fairly certain that the olfactory clue was really being used because, when the smell was very weak, the animal would press its nose right down onto the air outlet and draw in a prolonged sniff, just as though it was investigating a mouse hole. This also helped to remove any doubt as to the actual concentration of the odourous material in the air stream that entered the animal's nose. These threshold determinations are therefore probably more reliable than those of Moulton, for example, where the odourant was presented in solution, and the concentration in the air over the dish had to be estimated indirectly by calculation.

With his apparatus, Neuhaus found (as mentioned already on page 44) that for some substances the dog's olfactory threshold is not very different from man's, but that for others it may be very much lower: more than a million times lower for butyric acid and the other aliphatic acids.

Threshold
(molecules per c.c. of air)

Acid	Man	Dog
Acetic acid	$5 \cdot 0 \times 10^{13}$	$5 \cdot 0 \times 10^5$
Propionic acid	$4 \cdot 2 \times 10^{11}$	$2 \cdot 5 \times 10^5$
Butyric acid	$7 \cdot 0 \times 10^9$	$9 \cdot 0 \times 10^3$
Valeric acid	$6 \cdot 0 \times 10^{10}$	$3 \cdot 5 \times 10^4$
Caproic acid	$2 \cdot 0 \times 10^{11}$	$4 \cdot 0 \times 10^4$
Caprylic acid	$2 \cdot 0 \times 10^{11}$	$4 \cdot 5 \times 10^4$

These are very significant figures, because these aliphatic acids are known to be present in the skin secretions of both mammals and men. Neuhaus then went on to reason as follows.

There are several sources of skin secretions: sweat glands, 'odour glands', fat glands, and various others. The sole of the foot has only sweat glands, but they are present in large numbers: up to 1000 per square centimetre. Therefore the sweat glands are likely to be the most important. Over a period of 24 hours, the human body secretes about 800 c.c. of sweat, and from the two million or so sweat glands on the sole of each foot, about 2 per cent of the daily production, or about 16 c.c., would be released. Human sweat has about 0·156 per cent acid of which about one-quarter is aliphatic. If only 1/1000 of this penetrates steadily through the sole and the seams of the shoe, it can be calculated that of an acid such as butyric acid, at least $2 \cdot 5 \times 10^{11}$ molecules would be left behind in each footprint. This is well over a million times the threshold amount for the dog, and could still give a detectable smell when dispersed in 28 cubic metres of air. Under natural conditions, the rate of evaporation of the deposited material would depend on the temperature and the absorbent properties of the ground, so that it would be quite possible for a dog to follow a trail as much as 24 hours old, if conditions were favourable.

Neuhaus remarked that the calculated deposition of fatty acids is also above the threshold for perception by man, so that it should be possible for a man to follow a really fresh trail. To prove this, he laid sheets of clean blotting paper on a wooden parquet floor and had someone walk over it at normal speed. Approximately 30 seconds later, the sheets were given to a second person who was able to identify with certainty and by smell alone, the places where the footprints were.

Butyric acid is not the only contributor to the scent for there are at least ten other aliphatic acids present, as well as members of other chemical classes, including probably indoxyl and other indole compounds, phenols, biacetyl, and several others. In his later experiments, Neuhaus modified his apparatus so as to present to the dog not just a single odourant in the air stream, but a more or less complex mixture of odourants.

The results of these experiments were striking and suggestive.

For example, with mixtures of butyric acid with isovaleric or caproic acid, the threshold was much lower than the sum of the individual thresholds. He took this to indicate that the two odours had something in common which enabled them to reinforce each other synergistically. With entirely dissimilar odourants, such as butyric acid and alpha ionone, the threshold of the mixture corresponded approximately to the sum of the single thresholds. With a mixture of butyric acid and biacetyl, the threshold was intermediate —below the sum of the single thresholds but not as much below as with a mixture of two acids.

In another kind of experiment, the dog was asked to distinguish between a mixture of four aliphatic acids (propionic, butyric, iso-valeric, and caprylic) and an identical mixture containing a small addition of a fifth acid, caproic. It turned out that the dog could recognize a difference even when the concentration of caproic acid was substantially below its threshold for perception when smelled by itself. In other words, the character of a complex odour can be altered by sub-threshold amounts of impurities or trace constituents in the sample. When Neuhaus repeated the experiment with caproic acid added to a mixture of four very different smells (biacetyl, eugenol, ionone, and nerol), the amount of caproic acid required to alter the character had to be higher than its own threshold. Evidently in this mixture there was no significant common factor that the caproic acid could reinforce or build up, and so it had to exceed its own threshold to be noticed.

From all this work, Neuhaus concluded that the dog does not recognize the scent of an individual because of the presence of some one, single chemical substance peculiar to that person, but rather because of a pattern or complex to which substances may contribute even if they are present in sub-threshold amounts.

The theoretical aspects of this will be examined in a later chapter, but to anticipate just a little, it may be thought of as something like this.

The characteristic patterns of two similar substances, such as butyric and caproic acids, and of a dissimilar substance, such as ionone, might be pictured as follows:

Butyric acid: $--+-+--++ +---+-$ . . .
Caproic acid: $--+-----+++ +---++$ . . .
Ionone: $+----+----++ +---$ . . .

Evidently the two acids would be similar but not exactly identical, and in a mixture they could reinforce each other at many points. Ionone has nothing in common with the acids, and they would not act synergistically.

If the dog as a result of natural selection is adapted to tracking more than to general, all-round olfactory competence, its olfactory apparatus might be rather specialized for perceiving the pattern of substances associated with the sweat odour, and less fitted to discriminate contributors to the body odour that were not so specifically associated with the feet. Many observers have remarked on the curious fact that a dog can correctly identify a handkerchief that has been scented in the armpit after smelling the owner's hand, even though to us the odours are very different.

I think the most interesting and valuable thing about these experiments with dogs, and especially Neuhaus' measurements and calculations, is that they remove the performance from the realm of magic and make it depend neither on anything so ill-defined as 'instinct' or as uncanny as extra-sensory perception. To make a difficult and intricate phenomenon comprehensible is not to take something away from the phenomenon, but rather it is to add something to our own intellect.

It is also of some practical value. Dogs are regularly used by the police of many countries in the investigation of crime and the apprehension of criminals. If we understand how they perform their wonders, we can use them better and avoid possibly tragic mistakes. But a good tracking dog must be highly trained to follow the correct scent regardless of distractions and conflicting visual signs that could mislead a less well-trained animal. The tracking dog is a specialist, and must not be used for other purposes such as ordinary escort duty. Furthermore, Neuhaus is not alone in insisting that punishment was never used during the training of his experimental dogs. An animal that was ordinarily insensitive to a slap in the usual daily routine, reacted vigorously to the slightest punishment during the experiment and became unmanageable for the rest of the day. Oral aid was sufficient.

A good tracking dog is a precision instrument and must be treated like one.

REFERENCES

Anon. 'The Etiology of Misadventure', *J. Can. Med. Assn.*, **88**, 427–428, 1963. (Murphy's Law.)

F. BECKER, J. E. MARKEE, and J. E. KING. 'Studies of Olfactory Acuity in Dogs. (1) Discriminatory Behaviour in Problem Box Situations', *Brit. J. Animal Behaviour*, **5** (3), 94–103, 1957.

H. KALMUS. 'The Discrimination by the Nose of the Dog of Individual Human Odours and in Particular of the Odours of Twins', *Brit. J. Animal Behaviour*, **3**, 25–31, 1955.

H. KALMUS. 'Physiology and Genetics of Organoleptic Perception', in 'Molecular Structure and Organoleptic Quality'. S.C.I. Monograph No. 1, Society of Chemical Industry, London, 1957. pp. 13–27.

L. LÖHNER. (On the Individual and Regional Odour of Human Beings.) *Arch. ges. Physiol.* (Pflügers), **202**, 25–45, 1924.

L. LÖHNER. (Research on Olfactory Physiology; Olfactory Efficiency of Police Dogs.) *Arch. ges. Physiol.* (Pflügers), **212**, 84–94, 1926.

W. MCCARTNEY. 'Olfaction in Animals', *International Perfumer*, **4**, 3–10, 1951. (Includes quotation from Romanes.)

K. MOST. (Experiments with Human-Like but Non-Human Odour Trails.) *Hund.*, 469–475, 505–508, 1927.

K. MOST and G. H. BRÜCKNER. (On Hypotheses and Present Day Position on the Nasal Function of the Dog.) *Zentr. Kleintierk. Pelztierk.*, **12** (5), 9–30, 1936.

D. G. MOULTON, E. H. ASHTON, and J. T. EAYRS. 'Studies in Olfactory Acuity. 4. Relative Detectability of *n*-Aliphatic Acids by the Dog', *Animal Behavior*, **8** (3–4), 117–128, 1960.

W. NEUHAUS. (The Odour Thresholds of Dogs for Fatty Acids.) *Z. Vergl. Physiol.*, **35**, 527–552, 1953.

W. NEUHAUS. (The Discrimination of Odour Quantities by Men and Dogs in Experiments with Butyric Acid.) *Z. Vergl. Physiol.*, **37**, 234–252, 1955.

W. NEUHAUS. (The Odour Threshold of Odour-Mixtures for the Dog and Their Relation to the Thresholds for Unmixed Odours.) *Z. Vergl. Physiol.*, **38**, 238–258, 1956.

W. NEUHAUS. (The Ability of Dogs to Discriminate Mixtures of Odours.) *Z. Vergl. Physiol.*, **39**, 25–43, 1956.

W. NEUHAUS. (The Thresholds of Perception and Recognition in the Olfaction of the Dog in Comparison with the Olfactory Perception in Man.) *Z. Vergl. Physiol.*, **39**, 624–633, 1957.

W. NEUHAUS. (Differences in the Acuteness of Olfaction in Dogs.) *Z. Vergl. Physiol.*, **40**, 65–72, 1957.

11

Information Scenter

YOU are given a series of jars and asked to identify their contents by smell. You sniff them one by one and call out the result: tobacco—peppermint—soap—vanilla—roses—gasoline—sweat—ammonia—fish—chocolate—rotten eggs—lavender—rubber—smoke—pine oil—fresh bread—a horse—and so on.

The question is, how far on?

Almost anyone could extend the list very considerably and refine each of the items by specifying, for example, what kind of smoke: cigarette smoke, cigar smoke, wood smoke, coal smoke, oil smoke, etc. If you are a trained perfume chemist you could probably recognize quite a large number of grades of rose perfume, that is to say, a great many distinct though similar smells coming under the general classification of rose, which you might call one sub-division of a still larger class of flowery odours. If you are a professional fish-smeller (they do exist) you will make your living by judging the freshness and quality of fish and hence the price to be paid for them.

Taking it all round, it seems likely that the average person would have no trouble in distinguishing between several thousand odours, and an experienced authority in the field has claimed the ability to recognize well over ten thousand. Still another has simply said that the number is apparently unlimited.

It would be an interesting exercise to design an experiment to verify these estimates.

If, as we have seen, a dog can apparently distinguish between any two randomly selected persons (even including identical twins, though they would be more troublesome), I suspect that the actual number of discriminable odours is very large, and that ten thousand is a very low estimate. Now, when we identify a thing, we are not only saying what it is but we are also specifying all the things it is not, which means that we must procure and process a certain amount of information about it.

For example, suppose I show you an array of miscellaneous objects and tell you I am thinking about one particular one of them. You are to find out which one by asking questions I can answer by nodding my head or not nodding it. (I don't have to shake it to say 'no'. If I can say 'yes' or nothing, then saying nothing is the same as saying no.) You could find the right object by running through the array one by one, saying 'Is it this?', 'Is it this?', 'Is it this?' until you came to the right one, but that would be inefficient. You will get the right result much quicker if you are systematic.

You might draw a line through the array so that half the objects are on one side of the line and half are on the other. Then if you ask, 'Is it on this side of the line?' whether I nod or not the one question will have eliminated half the possibilities. If there are 8 objects, three questions is all you need because if you divide 8 by 2 three times you end up with 1. If there are 16 objects you need four questions, and for 32 you need five. If there are 1,048,576 objects, only twenty questions properly asked are needed to locate the chosen one.

Communications engineers, whose job it is to design telephone and other communication systems as efficiently as possible, have developed a general theory, known as information theory, which includes the kind of thing we are talking about. They measure information in 'bits', one 'bit' being the amount of information needed to reduce the uncertainty by half. The capacity of a 'channel' is the number of 'bits' of information it can transmit in one second.

Suppose there are 8 possible objects, any one of them can be designated by 3 bits of information. If it takes you one second to ask a question, and if I answer it by nodding my head or not nodding it during the next one second, then the capacity of the communication channel between us is 1 bit every 2 seconds, or half a bit per second. At that rate, it would take you 6 seconds to identify 1 out of 8 ($= 2^3$) objects, 10 seconds to identify 1 out of 32 ($= 2^5$) objects, and 40 seconds to identify 1 out of 1,048,576 ($= 2^{20}$). This would be true as long as I signal you by doing something or not doing it in the allotted time: nodding or not nodding, saying 'yes' or saying nothing, pressing a button or not pressing it, and so on. In other words, the signal may be transmitted by a beam of light from my head to your eyes, or by a sound wave when I say 'yes', or by an electrical impulse when I tap a key. If we know the capacity of a channel in bits per second, then we know something about the channel whether it is a beam of light, or a copper wire, or a nerve fibre.

You may feel that all this is highly artificial, and that it is neither possible nor necessary to bother about the informational content of the word 'darling' murmured in your ear. And indeed, this will usually be so because the number of words likely to be so murmured is rather small, and there is not likely to be much attenuation of the sound before it reaches you, and one hopes, too, that the surroundings will be fairly quiet. But if the speaker is on the far side of a busy street, it might be vital to know how many repetitions would be needed to make sure it was 'darling' and not 'darn thing', or that the message was not meant for you at all but for somebody named Sparling standing behind you.

What all this has to do with smells and smelling is quite simple and highly important. If your nose can identify any one out of ten thousand or more odours, and do it in a single sniff lasting about half a second, then it must have a certain informational capacity. Fourteen bits of information will identify any one of 16,384 possibilities ($2^{14} = 16,384$) and if any one of them can be identified in one half second the capacity of the channel is *at least* 28 bits per second. Our smelling apparatus must have a certain minimum degree of complexity to meet this requirement. It may have more than this minimum channel capacity, but it cannot have less. If it has more than the minimum it provides what the engineers call 'redundancy' which is useful as insurance against error and as a means of overcoming noise. ('Darling' sounds better when said more than once, and it may have to be said several times if the surroundings are noisy and if we are to be sure it is not 'Carling'.)

What qualities must our smelling organs have to give a minimum capacity of 28 bits per second? To answer this question we need to know certain things about nerves and nerve impulses.

A nerve is something like an electrically conducting wire, but it is made of a rather dilute salt solution instead of metal. The main consequence of this difference is a high electrical resistance in the nerve so that a very short piece of nerve acts like a very long piece of wire. An electrical impulse fed into a conductor tends to spread out and get smudged as it is conducted along, in something the same way that words shouted into one end of a long pipe come out the other end as a more or less inarticulate roaring or booming sound. To prevent this, telephone and telegraph engineers instal 'repeaters' or relays in the lines, and nature has provided nerves with devices called 'nodes of Ranvier' which serve the same purpose. For technical reasons connected with its structure as an elongated salt solution and the operation of the 'repeater' nodes, a single nerve fibre either carries an impulse or it does not. The response is all-or-nothing, not more-or-less. This can be shown by attaching wires to exposed nerves and actually measuring the signals as they go past. When this is done, the impulse is seen to be a brief pulse of electrical energy, often called a 'spike potential' from the way it looks on an oscilloscope. The spike lasts something less than 1/100 second, and after it has gone past the nerve must 'rest' for a certain length of time before it can transmit another pulse or spike. The 'refractory period' lasts for about 1/20 second so that a single nerve fibre can transmit no more than about 20 pulses per second.

One nerve fibre therefore has an informational capacity of only about 20 bits per second if we consider 'pulse' or 'no pulse' to be equivalent to the 'nod' and 'no nod' of the elementary guessing game I described earlier. To send a message of 14 bits we might use a single channel or nerve and transmit a series of 14 pulses or blanks, something like this:

$$+ + + - + - - - - + + - - +$$

If the capacity of the channel is 20 bits per second we would need almost three-quarters of a second to transmit a 14-bit message once. This kind of transmission uses what is called serial coding, and it is rather slow.

We could double the speed of the transmission by having two nerves and sending half the 'message' over one nerve and the other half simultaneously over the other. However, this would be complicated in that the message would have to be divided in some systematic way and there would have to be a fairly complicated receiving apparatus to put it together again.

It seems much more reasonable to suppose that if we are to be equipped with a smelling apparatus able to register, say, 16,384 ($= 2^{14}$) distinct odours, we will be equipped with not less than 14 types of sensory organ each capable of registering a different elementary olfactory quality. Then, by connecting each type of sensory organ with a direct line to headquarters, we can 'turn on the display' in 2^{14} or 16,384 different ways corresponding to the 16,384 separate odours it is required to recognize. This would actually provide much more than the required minimum channel capacity because a different complete 'picture' or pattern of spike potentials could be sent every 1/20 second. However, redundancy is within limits a good thing if we are to avoid error and especially if the channel is noisy.

Thus the known informational capacity of our sense of smell suggests that the smelling organ has something *more* than 13 or 14 kinds of end organ, and that each kind responds to a different kind of elementary or 'primary' odour. The situation is therefore rather more complicated than our perception of colour where only three primary colours will do. On the other hand, it is less complicated than sound where the number of pure tones that can be discriminated is well over 100. (The piano, which does not play intervals smaller than a semitone and which plumbs neither the highest nor the lowest tones our ears can hear, nevertheless has 88 keys.)

It is fairly easy to classify colours on a 'trichromatic' scale. No such system is possible with sounds, and despite many attempts, there are no good systems for describing or classifying odours. This is hard to explain if there are only a few primary odours, but it is only to be expected if there is a fairly large number of them. That probably explains the lack of success of odour-classification systems such as that of Crocker and Henderson which had 4 primary smells, or Henning's which had 6, or Zwaardemaker's which had 9. To discriminate ten thousand distinct odours needs just over 13 bits of information, and that would not include any provision for registering the strength of the smell—only its quality or identity. To allow for the need to transmit quantitative as well as qualitative information, and to allow for random imperfections and accidental false signals ('noise') in the system, we must allow some excess capacity or redundancy in the channel. That is, we should provide for the transmission of rather more 'bits' than is strictly necessary.

As I showed earlier, 20 bits can designate any one of 1,048,576 possibilities, and 25 bits will provide for more than thirty million. A very simple animal, such as a small insect, might be able to do very well with a smelling apparatus sensitive to only one primary smell, such as a sex-attractant. If the smell is perceived the insect can respond appropriately, and if it is not there is no need to burden the insect with the ability to contemplate all the irrelevant smells that attract other creatures.

A more complex animal might need an olfactory apparatus of somewhat higher informational capacity. A honey bee, for example, needs to be able to recognize one patch of flowers out of several, but it has no need to discriminate sardines from cheese. If the bee can distinguish 6 primary odours it can register and recognize 2^6 or 64 combination odours. This might be just enough and may be taken as the minimum. The maximum for bees is not likely to be much over 10 or 11 primaries which would provide the capacity to distinguish a few thousand kinds of flowers ($2^{10} = 1024$).

In the dog or some other richly endowed creature, the number of primary odours is likely to be in the range 25 to 35 which would enable it to distinguish many millions of smells, even with a certain amount of redundancy in the channel. As we will see in the next chapter, the microscopic examination of the olfactory tissues shows that its structure is consistent with the requirements of information theory, and there is a very interesting hint that in the rabbit the number of end-organ types (and hence the number of primary odours) is twenty-four—which would be about right.

This application of communications-engineering principles to the problem of smell is comparatively new. It was done in the first

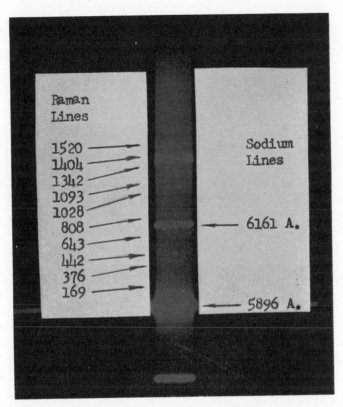

The Raman Spectrum of alpha Nitrothiophene

This photograph shows the spectrum of light from a sodium lamp scattered sideways by liquid nitrothiophene. In addition to the two wave lengths present in the sodium light (6161 and 5896 A) there are lines, some of them very faint, representing frequencies not present in the sodium lamp source. These are the Raman lines, and their frequency separation from the exciting (5896 A) sodium line gives the vibrational frequencies of the nitrothiophene molecules. The difficulty of seeing Raman lines below 169 wave numbers is evident. The picture was taken with a Hilger $f/4$ Raman spectrograph, with sodium light and a 2-hour time exposure. This compound is quickly decomposed by light of shorter wave length, and even sodium light generates fluorescence that produces a continuous background.

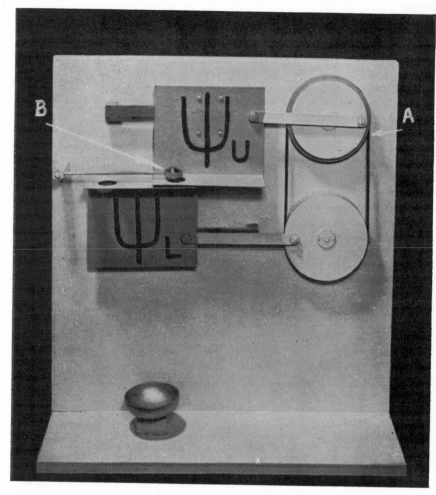

A Mechanical Analogue to the Transition Moment Integral

The two wave functions are represented by metal plates which are moved back and forth by cranks driven by pulleys of the same diameter (*A*), and which therefore oscillate with the same frequency. The plates each have a hole placed so that a steel ball (*B*) can fall through only when the two plates are at the same extreme of their motion at the same time (in phase); and as long as the condition shown in this picture continues the ball will not be allowed to fall.

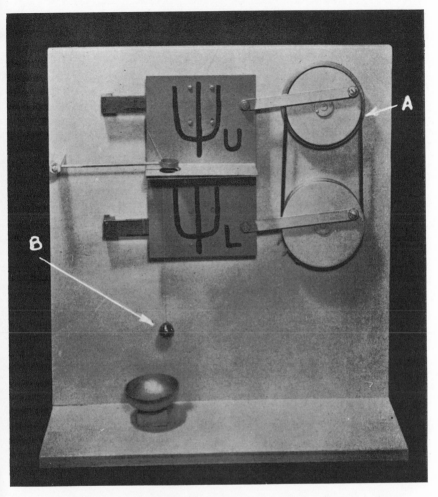

A Mechanical Analogue to the Transition Moment Integral (*contd.*)

If the size of one of the pulleys (*A*) is altered, the two oscillators have different frequencies as they move back and forth. The faster oscillator will gain on the slower, and they will pass in and out of phase. Whenever they are in phase, the return of the steel ball to the lower level will be allowed.

instance by R. M. Hainer and his co-workers in the United States and has served to clear away much muddled thinking and clarified many obscure points such as the long-standing absence of a satisfactory way to classify and describe odours. It explains, too, why a chemical that evokes a powerful response in a gypsy moth may have little or no odour to man.

If a dog can perceive twenty-five primary odours where we can perceive only twenty-four, there must evidently be at least one primary odour we cannot detect. In an earlier chapter I showed some evidence that in certain cases, such as butyric acid, the dog does smell something we do not. If there can be one such smell there can be several, and so it is not surprising that a thing that smells strongly to us may be odourless to a silk worm, and *vice versa*. What is more, things that are similar to us may or may not be similar to another animal.

REFERENCES

E. C. CROCKER and L. F. HENDERSON. 'Analysis and Classification of Odours', *Am. Perfumer and Essent. Oil. Rev.*, 22, 325–7, 356, 1927.

R. M. HAINER, A. G. EMSLIE, and A. JACOBSON. 'An Information Theory of Olfaction', *Ann. N.Y. Acad. Sci.*, 58, Art. 2, 158–174, 1954.

H. HENNING. (Smell; a Handbook for the Spheres of Psychology, Physiology, Zoology, Botany, Chemistry, Physics, Neurology, Ethnology, Language, Literature, Aesthetics, and History.) 2nd Ed., 434 pp., Leipzig, 1924.

J. R. PIERCE. *Symbols, Signals and Noise; the Nature and Process of Communication*. Harper & Bros., New York, 1961.

W. A. H. RUSHTON. 'Peripheral Coding in the Nervous System', in *Sensory Communications, A Symposium*. W. A. Rosenblith, Editor. M.I.T. Press, Wiley, New York, 1961. pp. 169–181.

H. ZWAARDEMAKER. (The Physiology of Smell.) Barth, Leipzig, 1924.

12

Tissues and Fibres

AN anatomist who makes a microscopic study of the sensory equipment of the nose is like a giant a mile high who wanted to study the communication network of London or New York. He could begin by imbedding the whole thing in wax, and then cut thin slices out of it in various directions. If his technique was good enough, he might get the thickness of the slices down to about ten feet, and with the best optical devices he might contrive to view the slices from the equivalent of a hundred yards distance. He might even be able to do some dissection of the slices, but his instruments would be no more delicate than a baseball bat or a broad-axe. By using colours that would soak into a plaster or concrete but not into metal or glass, he could trace the general outline of the various structures from one slice to the next.

In another kind of experiment, our giant could explore various civic functions and activities by destroying a traffic artery here or some other centre of activity there, and watching for signs of congestion or decay in nearby areas.

From all this, and with time, patience, thought, insight, and money (for equipment), he might eventually come to have a fairly good, rather broad understanding of the communications system of a modern city. He would probably never know the detailed structure of a dial telephone, but he would be pretty sure there was such a thing. He would realize that besides the telephone system there are postal and parcel delivery systems, and he would at least partly disentangle the specialized alarm systems that send warnings of fires and violent crimes to the appropriate action centres.

These techniques are all similar to those used by histologists and physiologists, and our noses have parallels for all these activities. Along with the sense of smell with its enormous informational capacity, there is the blood supply which nourishes and repairs, and there are receptors for heat and cold (which can respond also to certain chemicals like camphor and menthol), and a 'common chemical sense' that gives what is essentially a pain reaction with harmful or corrosive chemicals like formaldehyde or ammonia. These all have their own nerve systems which are just as distinct and just as closely tangled as the power, telephone and telegraph wires of a city which are often strung on the same poles. If this was not enough to complicate the anatomist's problems, our brain tends to

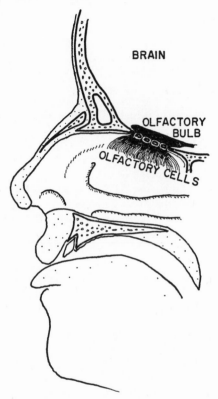

This picture shows the location of the olfactory cells in the upper part of the nasal passage.

fuse the messages from all these senses into a single complex sensation before presenting it to our consciousness, and the result is not easy to analyse.

The resemblance between the anatomist sorting out the sensory apparatus of the nose and a giant studying slices of New York 10 feet thick is accurate enough to explain why there are still more questions than answers. The microscopic anatomy of seeing and hearing are known in much more detail partly because to a man (if not to a dog) they are much more important senses, and also because the structures are larger and easier to study. Smelling takes place at the molecular level, and the structures are scaled down accordingly.

To make matters even more difficult, in man and the higher animals, the olfactory apparatus is located in the upper part of the nasal passage, roughly between the eyes and very close to the brain. This makes it rather inaccessible to study and observation in the living animal, and *post-mortem* examination is likely to be confused by the fact that the whole area is constantly open to infection by air-borne germs so that pathological abnormalities are very common while the animal is alive, and the moment it dies degenerative changes set in very quickly indeed. Much of the fine detail may be destroyed within an hour of death, and for this reason much less is known about the human olfactory structures than about those of the frog or rabbit, or certain fishes.

Before we leave the analogy of the communication network in our noses and that of a large city, there is one more lesson to be drawn from it. The tasks of repair and maintenance must go on as long as the city lives or the system soon breaks down. This is true also of the living sense organs, which may explain why they are made of such (to an engineer) exotic materials as jelly and salt solution. When something goes wrong with a telephone system, the defective component can be pulled out and replaced by a prefabricated spare. The body cannot do this with its broken or defective parts. They have to be dismantled and replaced a molecule at a time, and for this purpose the fluids and jellies of living tissue are actually better than copper wire and plastic would be. At the same time, the fact that these are the materials of construction in part determines the form the structure takes.

A nerve is essentially an elongated tube of jelly with one kind of salt solution inside it and another kind bathing the outside. The two salt solutions contain electrically charged ions which do not all diffuse through the membraneous walls of the nerve with the same ease. As a result of the difference in the diffusion rates of ions with $+$ and $-$ charges, an electric potential is set up between the inside and outside of the nerve. If this potential is somehow discharged momentarily so that the membrane is locally depolarized, the depolarization spreads to the adjoining parts of the membrane, and this goes on progressively so that a wave of depolarization flashes along the fibre. This is the 'spike potential' or nerve impulse. The membrane is not partly discharged: it swings all the way or not at all. Also, after the impulse has gone by it takes a certain time for the membrane potential to be re-established, and until that has happened the nerve cannot transmit another impulse. The all-or-nothing nature of the impulse and the refractory period that follows it were referred to in the last chapter. If the initial stimulation happens near the middle of the fibre the impulse travels off in both directions. In the ordinary way this would not do, for signals are supposed to go only one way at a time, and to avoid this nerves are interrupted at intervals by junctions or 'synapses' which have the property of passing signals in one direction only.

All this is fairly well understood. What is not so well known is the detailed mechanism of the primary stimulating process. We know that it involves a localized depolarization of the cell membrane, but how it becomes depolarized is still not clear. In some cases it may possibly be a mechanical bending that changes the ion-permeability of the jelly. (Our sensations of touch or hearing may perhaps be initiated in this way.) In other cases it might be a direct chemical action on the cell wall, as when salt is rubbed into a wound. In still others, such as sight, it could be a chemical change in or close to the cell wall brought about by radiant energy from far away. Where smell is concerned, we simply do not know what property of the odourous molecule enables it to trigger a nerve impulse: we only know it does. In a later chapter I will look at some current hypotheses, but they are still no more than that.

For the moment, let us consider only the structural anatomy of the smelling apparatus, leaving out the supporting structures, the blood vessels, and the heat-cold-and-pain-sensing elements that are entangled with it.

The end-organs that actually encounter the odourous molecules in the inspired air and where the primary sensations are generated are nerve cells of a special type. A nerve cell is a roughly tubular gelatinous bag with salt solutions inside and out. Somewhere inside the cell there is a structure called the nucleus from which the activities of the cell seem to be regulated, and there is usually an enlargement of the cell at that point which is called the cell body. Olfactory cells are bi-polar, which means that extensions run off in only two directions from the cell body.

The extension that runs from the cell body towards the actual sensing elements is a cylindrical, rod-like structure about 1 micron in diameter (1 micron = 1/1000 millimetre) and 20 to 90 microns long, so that it reaches to and perhaps a little beyond the actual surface of the olfactory epithelium. At the end of the rod there is a little enlargement called the olfactory vesicle, and radiating out from the vesicle there are several very minute, hair-like structures less than 0·2 microns in diameter. (It takes an electron microscope to see them properly because an optical microscope is limited in what it can resolve by the wavelength of light. The limit is around 0·2 microns.) The number of these thread-like cilia varies from 9 to 16 in the rabbit, and there is some doubt about their length. The older reports describe them as being only about 2 microns long, but more recent work has shown that in the frog and pig, the cilia extend out for 3 or 4 microns and then turn off at right angles and run parallel to the surface for possibly as much as 200 microns. They must therefore form a web or mesh of nerve fibres covering the whole surface of the olfactory organ, and so must provide a remarkably intimate contact between the odourous molecules and the actual substance of the nerve cells.

At its other end, each nerve cell narrows down to form a very fine fibre or axon which extends from the cell body through a thin, perforated bone (called the cribriform plate) into the brain cavity. Each sensory cell therefore has a direct line into the olfactory bulb of the brain. This is interesting because it is one of the things that the principles of information theory would lead us to expect, and would be consistent with a 'parallel coding' or 'bits' of information originating in a number of different types or end organ.

There is actually some indication that the olfactory end-organ cells are of more than one kind. The most significant is an observation by Drs. Beidler and Tucker who attached micro-electrodes to the olfactory epithelium of an oppossum at several places and showed that an odourous chemical which produced a strong discharge at one location produced a weak discharge at another, and other chemicals gave the reverse effect. They could not make electrodes small enough to connect to one olfactory cell at a time, but they were able to work with fairly small groups of cells. There are differences, too, in the way different cells accept the coloured stains which microscopists use to bring out different structures. This may mean something or it may not. Finally, the rod-like extension outward from the cell body to the vesicle where the hairs are attached varies from one cell to another, but this may be no more than a device to permit close packing of the cells in the epithelium.

So far, then, the picture is fairly clear. A large number of sensory cells broadly similar but not all identical make direct contact with the odourous molecules at one end, and at the other end each cell has its own direct axon to the olfactory bulb. Inside the olfactory bulb the microscope reveals a tangled web of axons, but each axon eventually ends up in a body called a glomerulus.

In the rabbit there are about 50 million primary olfactory cells on each side, and 50 million primary axons leading into the corresponding olfactory bulb on that side. In each olfactory bulb there are about 1900 glomeruli, so that on the average there will be about 26,000 primary cells connected to each glomerulus.

From the glomeruli, other nerve cells, called 'mitral cells' lead off to the olfactory centres of the brain, and there are about twenty-four such cells leading out of each glomerulus (in the rabbit). Hainer, Emslie, and Jacobson have suggested that the glomeruli function somewhat after the fashion of telephone exchanges (though A.R.P. 'filter centres' might be a closer parallel); and that signals from a large number (26,000) primary cells of twenty-four types feed into the glomeruli and are there sorted out so that all the signals from one type of primary sensor are combined and fed into a single output channel. (The twenty-four mitral cells leading out of the glomeruli is taken to indicate that twenty-four types of signals are being fed into them.) There is so far no experimental proof that this is the way the apparatus really works, and nothing to prove it is not.

What can be said is that their theory is based on sound engineering principles, and that it is consistent also with what is known both of the physiology of nerves and the anatomy of the olfactory system. It fulfils also one of the functions of a theory in that it suggests some lines of enquiry that might not have been thought of otherwise.

This has been a most elementary and incomplete account both of the anatomical details and of Hainer's consideration of it in terms of information theory. I have omitted many of their intriguing suggestions and refinements, such as the possible physical basis of the Weber-Fechner Law.

In the rabbit the total number of olfactory cells is about 100 million. If each carries 12 cilia or olfactory hairs, and if the hairs are 100 microns (0·01 cm.) long and 0·15 micron (0·000015 cm.) in diameter, they will have a combined surface area of nearly 600 square centimetres or approximately 100 square inches. This is the primary zone of contact between the odourous molecules and the sensory surface, the counterpart of the branching antennae of an insect. It is noteworthy that the sensory surface is the actual, bare substance of the nerve itself. In the eye there is a lens between the nerve and the outside environment and in the ear there is a tympanum. When we smell something we are making our most direct and intimate contact with the world. What is more, as we go inward from the olfactory epithelium we find only one nerve junction or synapse (in the glomerulus) between the primary sensitive surface and the olfactory centres of the brain. A more direct channel to the outside world would be hard to imagine.

Sir Wilfrid Le Gros Clark remarks that, 'I should perhaps emphasize that the olfactory bulb, in which the olfactory nerve fibres terminate, is developmentally an extension forwards of the cerebral hemisphere, and that the direct connexion with it of the olfactory receptors is taken to be an expression of the fact that, from the evolutionary point of view, the cerebral hemispheres were initially developed in the vertebrate series in relation to the olfactory sense.'

If the function of the brain is to regulate the activities of the organism on the basis of 'information received', it almost looks as though intelligence had its beginning as an apparatus for handling olfactory signals from the chemicals that bathed our first progenators in the primaeval ooze. If this is so, then Descartes' *'Cogito ergo sum'* (I can think, therefore I am) must yield priority to, *'Olfacio ergo cogito'* (I can smell and therefore I can think).

REFERENCES

A. C. ALLISON and R. T. TURNER WARWICK. 'Quantitative Observations on the Olfactory System of the Rabbit', *Brain*, **72**, 186–197, 1949.

G. BLOOM. 'Studies on the Olfactory Epithelium of the Frog and the Toad with the Aid of Light and Electron Microscopy', *Z. f. Zellforschung*, **41**, 89–100, 1954.

W. E. LE GROS CLARK. 'Observations on the Structure and Organization of Olfactory Receptors in the Rabbit', *Yale J. Biol. and Med.*, **29**, 83–95, 1956.

W. E. LE GROS CLARK. 'Inquiries into the Anatomical Basis of Olfactory Discrimination', *Proc. Roy. Soc.*, Ser. B, **146**, 299–319, 1957.

H. S. GASSER. 'Olfactory Nerve Fibres', *J. Gen. Physiol.*, **39**, 473–496, 1956.

R. M. HAINER, A. G. EMSLIE, and A. JACOBSON. 'An Information Theory of Olfaction', *Ann. N.Y. Acad. Sci.*, **58**, Art. 2, 158–174, 1954.

L. M. BEIDLER and D. TUCKER. 'Response of Nasal Epithelium to Odour Stimulation', *Science*, **122**, 76, 1955.

Y. ZOTTERMAN, Ed., *Olfaction and Taste*, MacMillan, New York, 1963.

13

How Strong is a Smell?

Once I wanted to know what a substance called phenyl acetylene smells like. I picked up Richter's *Organic Chemistry* and read on p. 446 that it is 'a liquid with a faint smell'. Bernthsen's *Organic Chemistry*, where I looked next, called it a 'fragrant liquid' on p. 414. Then I tried Dyson's *Manual of Organic Chemistry* and found on p. 157 that phenyl acetylene is 'a colourless liquid with an unpleasant smell reminiscent of leeks'. Later on I got a little sample of it and found that at full strength it smells much the way aromatic hydrocarbons generally do, and when somewhat diluted it was a little like nitrobenzene. However, I had not taken any precautions to purify it so that my observations mean very little.

Another time, I read a report that said a compound called benzyl bornyl ether smells like almonds. This was interesting, so I made a little of the compound and the product did smell like almonds—until I purified it carefully, when it had no smell at all.

This sort of thing is very common.

The technical journals contain many passing references to the smells of substances with no indication of how carefully they had been purified, or of how many people helped to describe the smell. This can be important because not everyone has the same olfactory capabilities. Hydrocyanic or prussic acid is commonly described as having an almond-like odour (though a few detective story writers say it is like violets). For a certain number of people (I am one) it is completely odourless, and this inability to smell it seems to be hereditary.

This is an example of 'partial anosmia' and there are other examples of it scattered through the technical journals. According to Blakeslee, verbena flowers are smelled differently by different people. It is likely that these differences are sometimes hereditary, and it would be interesting to trace the trait through several generations with a sharp look-out for correlations with other physical peculiarities such as blood-groupings or allergies.

Apart from the hereditary differences, there are differences connected with the physical state of the person doing the smelling. One observation, reported by M. Guillot in France, might have some

93

practical applications. A substance called exaltolide (15-hydroxy-pentadecanoic acid lactone) has a rather strong and somewhat unpleasant smell to women normally, but appears weak and faintly pleasant during pregnancy. Young children and men find it weak also, but this can be changed by administering the appropriate hormones.

This is probably connected with the fact that swallowing an odourous substance or injecting it subcutaneously can affect our ability to smell it. Working with dogs, Neuhaus found that when they were fed 1 gram of butyric acid or ionone, the first effect was to raise the olfactory thresholds for these substances so that the least concentration they could smell was twelve times greater than before. The thresholds then fell during several days and actually went below normal so that their sensitivity was as much as three times better than usual. It took 2 to 3 weeks for the animals to get back to normal after being given the chemical. Administering butyric acid did not affect the threshold for ionone, and *vice versa*. J. LeMagnen in France reported a similar effect with human subjects when various odourous substances were injected hypodermically.

Because of all these complications—impure samples, hereditary or acquired physical peculiarities, or the variability of the smell at different concentrations—casual or passing references to the odour of a compound mean almost nothing. Any discussion of the relation of odour to chemical constitution should take this into account, but not all of them have. We still find serious discussions based on trivial observations.

One erroneous piece of olfactory information was put on record by a man whose whole life work was devoted to smells and smelling, and not as a passing reference. The International Critical Tables (a careful compilation of all sorts of chemical and physical data) has a table of olfactory threshold concentrations that are all too low by a factor of 100. It was almost certainly due to a slip of the mind by a man too-familiar with the subject, but the strange thing is that although the tables were published in 1926, it was not until 1953 that attention was drawn to the error.

The chemistry of odours would be difficult enough even without these complications, and any discussion that took them all into account would be very, very tedious. I will therefore touch on only a few of the ways smell is related to chemical constitution.

The first thing to consider is the relation between the strength of an odour and the structure, molecular weight, volatility, or other properties of the odourous material.

The 'strength' of an odour can be expressed in various ways. One of the commonest is in terms of the threshold concentration, on the principle that a substance with a 'strong' odour will be smelled at a very small concentration. Much work has been done on this line, but it is not really very satisfactory because while it is true that odours can be identified as well as detected down to very low concentrations, nevertheless the threshold of detection and the threshold of identification are not exactly the same. Further than that, working near the threshold of perception is a niggling business and not much fun for anyone. Sometimes, after going through a lot of painstaking work, one runs into an embarrassing situation as when two very careful experimenters opened a fresh bottle of isopropanol and got thresholds that differed systematically by 400 per cent from the ones they had observed previously with another bottle of the same chemical bought from the same manufacturer.

Furthermore, threshold measurements are not necessarily the best measure of the 'strength' of a substance's smell. The odour of ethyl mercaptan can be made to vary all the way from just perceptible to overwhelmingly strong by changing the concentration. The threshold for musk or vanillin is much lower than that for ethyl mercaptan, but even at concentrations many thousands of times higher than threshold, their smells are still not very strong.

To distinguish between the two kinds of odour strength the words 'insistence' and 'insistent' are sometimes used to denote smells that are perceptible at very low concentrations but are not strong even at high concentrations.

One rather obvious explanation of the variation in insistence would be a difference in the size of the J.N.D. If a rather small change in the stimulus would make a just noticeable change in the sensation, then the sum of a large number of J.N.D.'s should add up to a strong odour. However, Gamble and others long ago showed that the J.N.D.'s are pretty constant, and camphor and vanillin, for example, appear to have much the same value for $\Delta x/x$ notwithstanding the fact that vanillin has one of the most insistent smells known while camphor has not.

On the Stevens system of measuring intensity (described in Chapter 7), the rate at which the smell 'grows' depends on the constant n in the formula,

$$S = x^n$$

So far only a few odours have been studied by the Stevens method. They were all substances of rather moderate insistence, and they all had values of n not far from 0·5. It would be a very good thing to make a systematic investigation of substances of very high insistency as well as substances with very high smell strength.

Because of the difficulties of working always near the threshold of perceptibility, an interesting new technique based on the Stevens system has been put forward for comparing smell strengths at concentrations well above threshold. To understand it, let us first look at another kind of experiment.

It is fairly easy for an observer looking at two white lights to judge whether they are approximately equally bright, and he can make the same sort of judgment of equality with weights held in his hand, or with two electric shocks, and so on. If, however, you are asked to say when a coloured light has the same brightness as a white one, or to judge when a high-pitched sound has the same loudness as a low-pitched one, then you are no longer comparing the same thing. Nevertheless, experiments show that respectable comparisons can be made in this way. What is even more curious, this kind of comparison (it is known technically as a 'cross-modality match') can be made even between such unrelated sensations as the loudness of a sound and the intensity of a vibration felt with the fingers. In fact, cross-modality comparisons have been carried out on a 'round robin' basis so as to complete—and close—a circle of comparisons.

This kind of matching is an extension of the Stevens process of 'ratio estimation'. If we have two sensations S_1 and S_2 (they might be light and sound for example) which are at the same level above threshold, then,

$$S_1 = \left(\frac{x_1}{x_0}\right)^n$$

$$S_2 = \left(\frac{y_1}{y_0}\right)^m$$

then if $S_1 = S_2$ as we assumed,

$$\left(\frac{x_1}{x_0}\right)^n = \left(\frac{y_1}{y_0}\right)^m$$

or,

$$\log\frac{x_1}{x_0} = \frac{m}{n}\log\frac{y_1}{y_0}$$

This means that the ratios between the stimuli will be the same, and this is just what the experiments show. In fact, the experiments in cross-modality matching were probably done in the first place to check this mathematical deduction from the simple observations of ratio estimation within a single modality.

The psychological or physiological reasons why this should happen are not known, but in terms of the nerve signals described in the last chapter it is not altogether surprising.

If a sensation is transmitted as a train of nerve impulses, two sensations that have the same ratio to their respective thresholds are likely to be occasioned by physically similar trains of spike potentials. Mathematically, if the 'spike frequency', n, corresponds to a sensation of strength I, and if n and I are logarithmically related like this,

$$n = a \log I$$
$$n_0 = a \log I_0$$

(I_0 is the threshold sensation), then

$$n - n_0 = a \log \frac{I}{I_0}$$

If two different sensations, I and J, have similar values for $(n - n_0)$, it will necessarily follow that

$$a \log \frac{I}{I_0} = b \log \frac{J}{J_0}$$

which is just what is observed in a cross-modality comparison.

Therefore the facts as observed would make sense *if* the logarithmic relation,

$$n = a \log I$$

does in fact exist. Without going into details, it turns out that this is just what information theory would require of a communication channel which is to maintain a constant ratio of signal to noise notwithstanding great changes in the average level of the stimulus.

I do not want to imply that the nerve anatomy and physiology were designed by Providence so as to have the maximum efficiency. That is the teleological view and it is quite out of fashion. All that I am saying is that the long-term effect of natural selection is to favour the survival and elaboration of whatever works the best.

But it is high time I got back to the relation (if any) of smell strength to chemical structure.

Taking Stevens as their point of departure, Kruger and his associates in the United States selected a substance, *n*-heptenal, which has a distinctive and inoffensive odour which they could use at full strength or dilute progressively with a substantially odourless solvent, benzyl benzoate. Bottles containing the various solutions could be presented to observers for strength evaluation by sniff tests.

Their observers were first 'trained' by presenting the bottles in random order and asking the observers to arrange them in order from the strongest to the weakest. When they could do that correctly every time, they proceeded to the second step, which was to match the strength of a *different* smell against one (or between two) of the smells in the standard series. Experiments showed that this could generally be done with an acceptable degree of reproducibility. Using this technique, they studied the way the odourous strength varies in a series of compounds of the same general chemical type, known as the normal primary aliphatic alcohols:

$$CH_3-CH_2-CH_2OH \quad \text{1-propanol}$$

$$CH_3-(CH_2)_2-CH_2OH \quad \text{1-butanol}$$

$$CH_3-(CH_2)_3-CH_2OH \quad \text{1-pentanol}$$

. . .   . . .

$$CH_3-(CH_2)_{10}-CH_2OH \quad \text{1-dodecanol}$$

First these alcohols were presented to the observers at full strength, that is undiluted with benzyl benzoate, and the strength of their several odours were compared with the various heptenal standards. It was found that each observer could reproduce his own judgments very well, but there were sometimes variations between the different observers, especially near the ends of the series. Two of the observers rated the odour of 1-propanol (three carbon atoms) as weaker than higher members of the series, and one found the odour of 1-dodecanol (twelve carbons) to be rather weak. Aside from these peculiarities there was agreement among the three judges that the strength of the odour diminished gradually as the molecular weight increased.

The experiment was repeated six times with the alcohols progressively diluted with more and more benzyl benzoate so as to reduce their odour strength and bring them lower and lower down on the heptenal scale. The results confirmed the general rule that from about C_4 on, the odour grew weaker with increasing molecular weight.

Since the high molecular weight members are less volatile than the others, the drop in intensity with molecular weight could be due simply to reduced volatility acting to reduce the number of odourous molecules entering the nose. To investigate this point they diluted the alcohols with benzyl benzoate so that the solutions would all have the same vapour pressure. When the decrease in molecular concentration of the vapour was compensated in this way, the longer chain length showed slightly higher odour intensity. Evidently this could become meaningless still higher up the series because the compound 1-eicosanol ($CH_3-(CH_2)_{18}-CH_2OH$) for example is odourless and its volatility is negligible. If the lower members of the series were diluted to the same very low volatility they would probably be too dilute to be smelled also, though the point should be checked experimentally to make sure.

The general conclusion from this is that when the members of a family of organic compounds of the same type (a homologous series) are compared without correcting to the same vapour pressure, the intermediate members with about five to eight carbon atoms are likely to have the strongest odours, and the lowest and highest members tend to be somewhat weaker—though probably for different reasons.

The method used by Kruger and his associates has much to recommend it and is likely to be used more and more in studies of this kind.

The smell strength of this same series of alcohols was studied by Moulton and Eayrs using rats instead of human subjects, and determining the threshold concentrations at which 50 per cent of their animals showed a positive response to the odour. They found that members of the series with five to eleven carbon atoms were approximately equally stimulating. The lower members were less stimulating and had higher thresholds.

Dethier and Yost, working with blowflies (*Phormia regina*), and the same group of chemicals, found that the flies avoided an air stream containing the chemicals at lower and lower concentrations as one went up the series, until the cut-off point was reached where the substances were simply not volatile enough to be perceived.

Thus the qualitative rule is fairly clear, and similar studies with other families of compounds show the same general result:

(1) When the members of a homologous series are smelled at full strength or at equal dilutions in an inert solvent and without correcting to equal vapour pressure, the smell rises to a maximum strength at somewhere around five or six carbon atoms and thereafter diminishes.

(2) When the members of a homologous series are smelled at equal vapour concentrations, the smell is stronger for the higher members until they are no longer volatile enough to reach the required vapour concentration. Here, again, the lowest members of the series are likely to be exceptional.

The exceptional behaviour of the lowest members has been explained in various ways. The commonest suggestion depends on the fact that to reach the olfactory end organ, an odourous molecule may have to be soluble in both the watery mucous and the fat-like lipid substances in the cell walls of the smelling apparatus. The first three members of the alcohol series are completely soluble in water and the rest are soluble only to a limited extent. This may affect their ease of access to the membrane.

So far so good.

We have two different and apparently distinct criteria of a 'strong' odour: one a low threshold, and the other a steep rise in the strength of the smell once the threshold has been passed. The exponent, n, in the Stevens formula may turn out to be a useful measure of the second of these (though it still has to be proved) and its theoretical interpretation can be postponed until then. The position is a little better as regards the olfactory thresholds. They have been tackled theoretically by J. T. Davies and F. H. Taylor in an interesting way, and the matter is important enough to be looked at rather carefully.

Since odours are perceived when the odorous molecules become temporarily stuck to the cell membrane (the technical word for this is adsorption), their theory begins there. The cell membrane is probably of a fatty or lipid nature but is bathed in a watery layer of mucus. The odorous molecules must therefore pass from the air into the lipid-water boundary layer and Davies and Taylor assume that the ordinary 'Partition Law' of physical chemistry will apply to the distribution of the molecules:

$$\frac{C_1}{C_a} = K_{1/a}$$

where C_1 is the average concentration of odorous molecules in the cell surface, and C_a is their concentration in the air, and $K_{1/a}$ is a constant called the partition coefficient which varies from one substance to another but is constant for any one substance whether C_a is large or small.

The term C_1 denotes the concentration in the surface layer expressed as molecules per *cubic* centimetre. To change this to the number of molecules per *square* centimetre of cell surface, they assume that the surface layer has a thickness, d, of about 1 millimicron (10^{-6} mm.) so that the average number of molecules per square centimetre of surface is C_1/d.

These molecules are not evenly spaced out over the cell surface any more than a handful of peas dropped on the ground from a height will be evenly spaced out. The distribution will be random, with places where the density of the adsorbed molecules is higher than average and others where it is lower. It is assumed that when the local density of the adsorbed molecules rises above a certain figure, the molecules can in some way discharge or 'puncture' the cell membrane, and some kinds of molecules are assumed to have a higher 'puncturing' power than others. To translate these rather general ideas into mathematical language, the surface of the cell membrane is imagined to be divided into small areas, or 'sites', which are small enough that the random distribution of the odourous molecules will give them a randomly varying population of adsorbed molecules.

This makes it a standard problem in probability theory for which there is a ready-made formula called Poisson's Equation:

$$\frac{N}{n} = \frac{e^{-aC_1}(aC_1)^p}{p!}$$

In this formula, a is the area of a 'site', and aC_1 is the average number of molecules per site; N is the number of sites containing a number, p, or molecules which is larger than the average, aC_1, and n is the total number of sites per cell.

To trigger a nerve impulse at least one site must have the critical number of molecules, so that the smallest possible value of N is 1. Also, the smallest possible number of odourous molecules per site is 1. (This would be the case for a very strong odourant with a maximum 'puncturing' ability.) For the weakest odourants the critical number per site might be 20 or 30. By combining the partition formula with Poisson's formula, and putting in the various constants, the ordinary operations of mathematics lead to the formula:

$$\log \text{O.T.} + \log K_{1/a} = \frac{-4 \cdot 64}{p} + \frac{\log p!}{p} + 21 \cdot 19$$

If the assumptions are reasonably correct, this should enable the olfactory threshold (O.T.) to be calculated if one knows the partition coefficient, $K_{1/a}$, and the value of p. The value of $K_{1/a}$ can be found for each substance by straightforward partition measurements of the odourous substance between oil (or fat) and water and between water and air.

The value of p is more difficult, because we do not know how the odourous molecules actually interact with the cell membrane so as to 'puncture' it. (I will look at some current theories in a later chapter.) Davies and Taylor think that it probably depends at least partly on the size and shape of the odourous molecules. Specifically, they suppose that a molecule as 'slim' as a water molecule will have no puncturing ability (because water has no smell) and that a molecule as 'fat' as beta ionone will have a maximum puncturing ability (because ionone has one of the lowest thresholds known), and that in between, puncturing power is a straight-line function of the cross-sectional area of the molecule.

From other experiments, we know something about the size and shape of various molecules, though in some cases we may have to guess whether a long-chain, thread-like molecule is more likely to be curled up or stretched out straight. To be on the safe side Davies and Taylor calculated it both ways whenever there was any doubt. For the normal primary alcohols (which we discussed earlier in this chapter) they have calculated the thresholds assuming both the coiled and the stretched-out configurations, and it is interesting to

Comparison of the calculated and observed olfactory thresholds
for the aliphatic primary alcohols

Threshold (molecules per c.c.)

Alcohol	Calculated (Davies and Taylor)		Man (Various observers)	Rat (Moulton and Eayrs)	Blow fly (Dethier and Yost)
	coiled	uncoiled			
C_3H_7OH	5×10^{13}	3×10^{14}	5×10^{13}	6×10^{14}	3×10^{16}
C_4H_9OH	8×10^{12}	1×10^{14}	8×10^{12}	3×10^{13}	4×10^{15}
$C_5H_{11}OH$	1×10^{12}	2×10^{13}	7×10^{12}	1×10^{12}	1×10^{15}
$C_6H_{13}OH$	1×10^{11}	8×10^{12}	7×10^{12}	2×10^{12}	2×10^{14}
$C_7H_{15}OH$	5×10^{10}	6×10^{12}	9×10^{11}	9×10^{11}	2×10^{14}
$C_8H_{17}OH$	4×10^9	1×10^{12}	3×10^{10}	7×10^{10}	1×10^{15}
$C_{10}H_{21}OH$	1×10^8	3×10^{11}	4×10^{11}	8×10^9	3×10^{14}

Comparison of calculated olfactory thresholds with thresholds
observed for man and for dog

Threshold (molecules per c.c.)

	Calculated (Davies and Taylor)		Observed	
	coiled	uncoiled	Man	Dog
Butyric acid	1×10^{10}	1×10^{11}	1×10^{11}	9×10^3
Valeric acid	1×10^{10}	4×10^{11}	1×10^{11}	4×10^4
Caproic acid	3×10^9	2×10^{11}	1×10^{12}	4×10^4
β Ionone	2×10^8	2×10^8	2×10^8	7×10^4

compare their values with those found by experiment. The results are shown in the table, and considering the difficulty of the problem and the rough-and-ready approximations that had to be made, the agreement with the experimental values is quite good. The blow flies seem to be less sensitive than they might be.

A disturbing fact turns up when we compare the predicted values with some of the observed thresholds for the dog. I pointed out in Chapter 7 that for the dog some thresholds are about 1000 times lower than for man, in which case we are probably smelling the same thing, but that there are other substances where the dog's threshold is more than a million times lower than ours, and here the dog is probably smelling something we do not. The thresholds Davies and Taylor calculate agree as well as can be expected with the human thresholds and the dog thresholds that correspond to them, but they are rather far out for the substances for which the dog threshold is very low. I do not think this necessarily upsets their theory, but it points to the existence of factors other than the 'fatness' or 'slimness' of the odourous molecules in determining their puncturing power.

REFERENCES

A. F. BLAKESLEE. 'Unlike Reactions of Different Individuals to Fragrance in Verbena Flowers', Science, 48, 298–299, 1918.

G. H. CHEESMAN and M. J. TOWNSEND. 'Further Experiments on the Olfactory Thresholds of Pure Chemical Substances, Using the Sniff Bottle Method', Quart. J. Exptl. Psychol., 8, 8–14, 1956.

J. T. DAVIES and F. H. TAYLOR. 'The Role of Adsorption and Molecular Morphology in Olfaction: the Calculation of Olfactory Thresholds', Biol. Bull., 117, 222–238, 1959.

V. G. DETHIER and M. T. YOST. 'Olfactory Stimulation of Blowflies by Homologous Alcohols', J. Gen. Physiol., 35, 823–839, 1952.

E. A. McC. GAMBLE. 'The Applicability of Weber's Law to Smell', Am. J. Psychol., 10, 82–142, 1898.

M. GUILLOT and A. FIEHRER. (Folliculin and Olfactory Sensation.) Compt. rend. Soc. Biol., 143, 922–923, 1949.

F. N. JONES. 'Olfactory Thresholds in the International Critical Tables', Science, 118, 333, 1953.

R. L. KIRK and N. S. STENHOUSE. 'Ability to Smell Solutions of Potassium Cyanide', Nature, 171, 698–699, 1953.

L. KRüGER, A. N. FELDZAMEN, and W. R. MILES. 'A Scale for Measuring Supra-Threshold Olfactory Intensity', Am. J. Psychol., 68, 117–123, 1955.

L. KRüGER, A. N. FELDZAMEN, and W. R. MILES. 'Comparative Olfactory Intensities of the Aliphatic Alcohols in Man', Am. J. Psychol., 68, 386–395, 1955.

D. G. MOULTON and J. T. EAYRS. 'Studies in Olfactory Acuity. II. Relative Detectability of n-Aliphatic Alcohols by the Rat', Quart. J. Exptl. Psychol., 12, 99–109, 1960.

W. NEUHAUS. (Odour Thresholds of Dogs for Ionone and Ethyl Mercaptan and their Relation to Other Odour Thresholds of Dog and Man.) Z. Naturforsch., 9b, 560–567, 1954.

W. NEUHAUS. (Variation of the Olfactory Acuteness of the Dog by Oral Administration of Odouriferous Substances.) Z. Vergl. Physiol., 41, 221–241, 1958.

J. LeMAGNEN. (Study of a Phenomenon of Olfactory Sensitization.) Compt. rend. Acad. Sci. Paris, 228, 122–124, 1949.

W. A. H. RUSHTON. 'Peripheral Coding in the Nervous System', in Sensory Communication, A Symposium. W. A. Rosenblith, Editor. M.I.T. Press, Wiley, New York, 1961, pp. 169–181.

S. S. STEVENS. 'The Psychophysics of Sensory Function', in *Sensory Communication, A Symposium*. W. A. Rosenblith, Editor. M.I.T. Press, Wiley, New York, 1961. pp. 1–33.

H. ZWAARDEMAKER. 'Odouriferous Materials', in *International Critical Tables*, **1,** 358–361, 1926. McGraw-Hill.

14

The Chemical Puzzle

I ONCE asked a chemist friend to smell two substances which most people regard as being rather similar, and to tell me what he thought about them. He sniffed them carefully and then declared roundly that they were entirely distinct, that he could tell them apart easily, *and therefore there was no similarity between them.* To his literal mind, there was no middle ground between two odours being identical and indistinguishable, and two odours having nothing in common at all. This is foolishness, of course, because as soon as we begin to compare smells we find that the middle ground is where we spend most of our time.

If I say that two compounds have a floral smell, I mean that they are as alike as, say, a violet is like a rose, and while no one would mistake the two, yet the smell of a violet is more like the smell of a rose than it is like the smell of a fish. Narrowing things down still further, if I say that two compounds have a rose-like odour, I do not mean that they are indistinguishable from a rose and from each other—I merely mean that there is a fairly close resemblance, but not an absolute identity.

I hope this is not labouring an obvious point, but in a good many discussions I have had to labour it—and belabour it—to avoid being misunderstood.

So much for one preliminary. Now for another.

A hundred years ago, Kekulé laid the foundation of modern organic chemistry by inventing structural formulae. He took the atomic and molecular theories of his day and added something new in the shape of an assumption that atoms need not always join themselves to atoms that are different from themselves, as in H—Cl or Ca=O, but that they could also join themselves to other atoms *of their own kind* so as to form 'chains' of atoms, and he assumed that carbon atoms have this capability exceptionally highly developed. With this as a basis, he and those who came after him have erected a magnificent structure theory by studying the chemical properties of organic substances and deriving from these studies 'structural formulae' which embody the properties in a pictorial way. Let me show how this is done in a simple case.

There is a colourless liquid whose quantitative composition and molecular weight correspond to the formula CH_4O. It reacts in various ways with a great many other chemicals, and out of all these varied reactions I will pick out two as being significant for my purpose. First, if you add a little piece of sodium to the liquid, it bubbles and reacts vigorously, hydrogen is released, and the end product is a white solid substance with the formula $NaCH_3O$. The reaction goes no farther than this, for there is no compound Na_2CH_2O. Evidently, then, in the original substance, CH_4O, one of the four hydrogen atoms can be replaced by sodium and the other three cannot. One of the four is somehow unique, or at least different. The second significant reaction is one with phosphorus trichloride, which converts CH_4O into CH_3Cl, and it is also significant that in CH_3Cl there is no longer a hydrogen atom that can be replaced by sodium.

So: in CH_4O one H atom is somehow different, and it and the oxygen atom can be replaced by a single atom of chlorine.

Now we know from general chemistry that atoms have certain characteristic combining capacities, or 'valences': hydrogen, 1; oxygen, 2; carbon, 4 (these values applying nearly always); and chlorine is usually 1, but occasionally something else in some of its compounds.

The simplest way to represent the properties of our compound, consistently with the usual valences of the atoms, is by this structural formula:

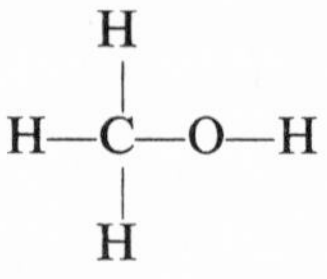

$$\begin{array}{c} H \\ | \\ H-C-O-H \\ | \\ H \end{array}$$

which makes one of the hydrogens different by being linked to O while the others are linked to C, and the 'different' H and the O can be removed together and replaced by a monovalent chlorine atom.

When we come across another compound, C_2H_6O, which reacts with sodium and with phosphorus trichloride in just the same way, we can assign it the formula,

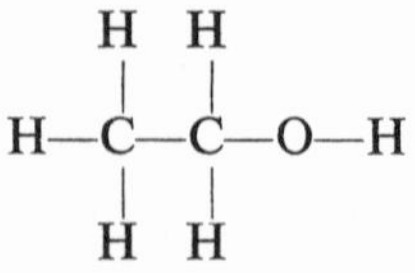

$$\begin{array}{c} H \quad H \\ | \quad | \\ H-C-C-O-H \\ | \quad | \\ H \quad H \end{array}$$

(remembering Kekulé's assumption about the chain-forming ability of carbon atoms).

The series can continue, and in fact in the last chapter I talked mainly about the higher members of this family, or 'homologous series' of the normal, primary, aliphatic alcohols. ('Normal' because the chains are not branched, 'primary' because the —OH is at the end, and 'aliphatic' because the chains do not form closed loops or rings.)

This is a rather long preamble to a discussion of whether smell can be related to the chemical structure, but I think it is necessary to see what a structural formula is—and how we know what it is—if the rest of this chapter is to make any real sense. The structure is deduced from the chemical properties, and while it is convenient to say that an alcohol reacts in certain ways 'because it has an —OH group', what we really mean is that we believe it to have an —OH group because of the way it reacts.

The immense success of structural organic chemistry results from the fact that structures can be systematically correlated with the chemical properties in this way, and when we have done it, we find that many physical properties (such as the optical refraction) and even some medicinal properties can be correlated too.

But there is a limit, and when we come to odours they simply will NOT correlate in any systematic or sensible way with the structures. Substances with quite different structures may smell much alike (always remembering that 'alike' is not necessarily the same thing as 'identical'). For example, these substances have a rose-like smell:

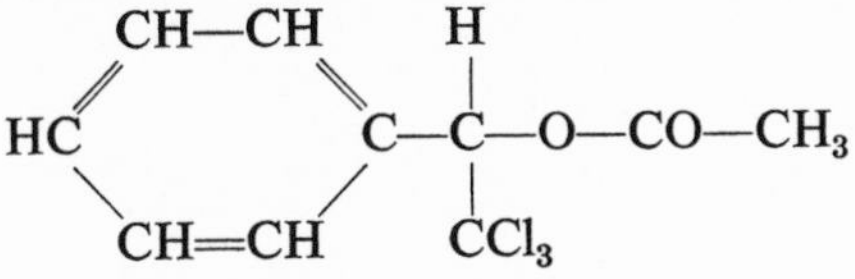

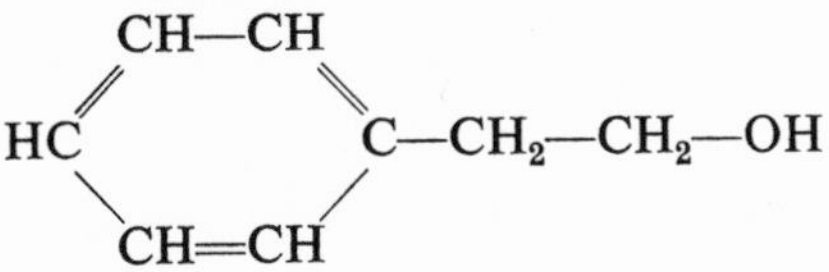

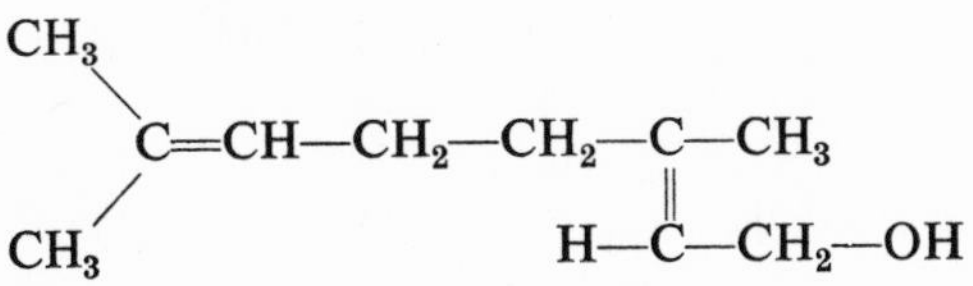

107

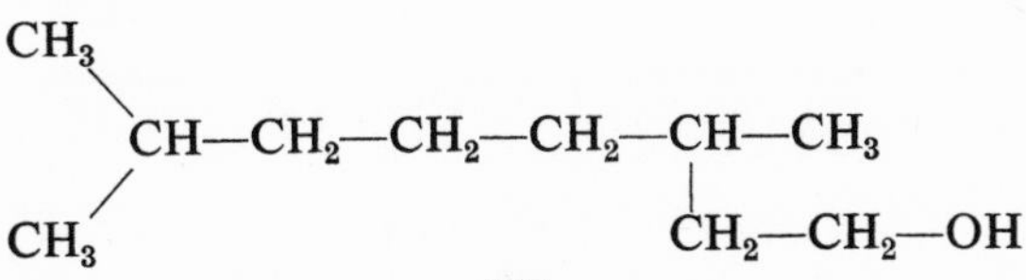

and these smell something like camphor:

'Camphor'
$$CH_2—\overset{\overset{\displaystyle CH_3}{|}}{C}—C=O$$
$$CH_3—\overset{|}{C}—CH_3$$
$$CH_2———CH———CH_2$$

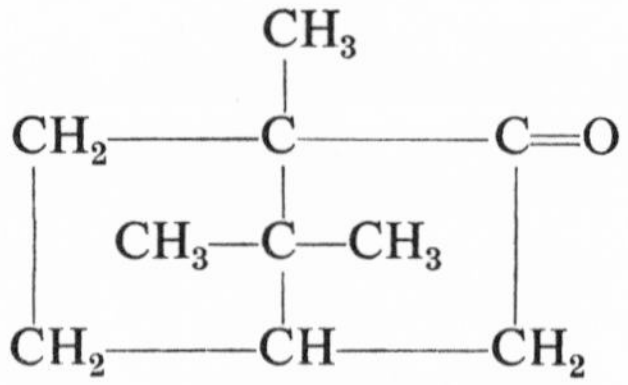

'Chloretone'
$$Cl—\overset{\overset{\displaystyle Cl}{|}}{\underset{\underset{\displaystyle Cl}{|}}{C}}—\overset{\overset{\displaystyle CH_3}{|}}{\underset{\underset{\displaystyle CH_3}{|}}{C}}—OH$$

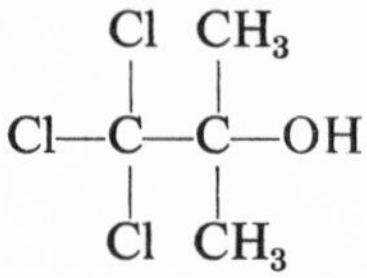

'Ethyl tert. butyl ether'
$$CH_3—CH_2—O—\overset{\overset{\displaystyle CH_3}{|}}{\underset{\underset{\displaystyle CH_3}{|}}{C}}—CH_3$$

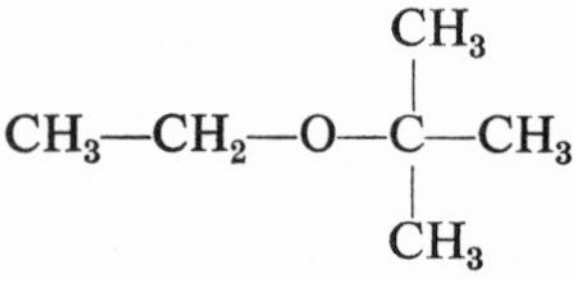

If things with very different structures can have very similar smells, the opposite is also true: things with rather similar structures may have more or less different smells, though if the structures are sufficiently alike the difference in smell is likely to be rather small. For example, von Braun and Kröper made this series of compounds:

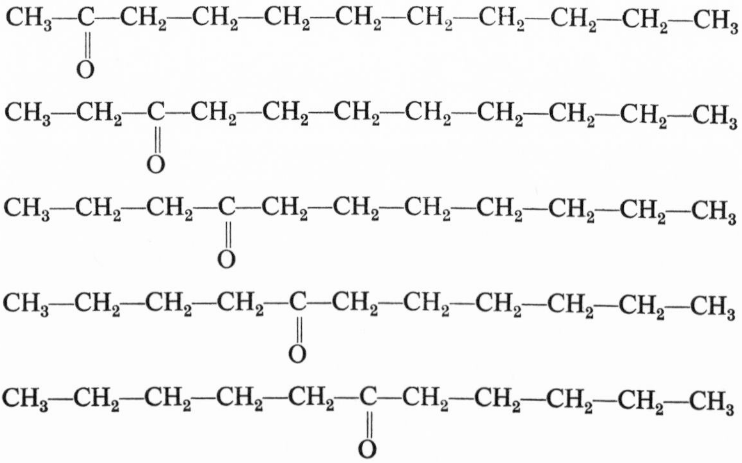

$$CH_3—\overset{\overset{}{\underset{\underset{\displaystyle O}{\|}}{C}}}{}—CH_2—CH_2—CH_2—CH_2—CH_2—CH_2—CH_2—CH_2—CH_3$$

$$CH_3—CH_2—\overset{\overset{}{\underset{\underset{\displaystyle O}{\|}}{C}}}{}—CH_2—CH_2—CH_2—CH_2—CH_2—CH_2—CH_2—CH_3$$

$$CH_3—CH_2—CH_2—\overset{\overset{}{\underset{\underset{\displaystyle O}{\|}}{C}}}{}—CH_2—CH_2—CH_2—CH_2—CH_2—CH_2—CH_3$$

$$CH_3—CH_2—CH_2—CH_2—\overset{\overset{}{\underset{\underset{\displaystyle O}{\|}}{C}}}{}—CH_2—CH_2—CH_2—CH_2—CH_2—CH_3$$

$$CH_3—CH_2—CH_2—CH_2—CH_2—\overset{\overset{}{\underset{\underset{\displaystyle O}{\|}}{C}}}{}—CH_2—CH_2—CH_2—CH_2—CH_3$$

They all had a somewhat rue-like smell, but it diminished and was largely replaced by a fruity odour as the —CO— group was moved in towards the middle of the chain.

Winter and Gautschi have recently prepared these two isomeric substances:

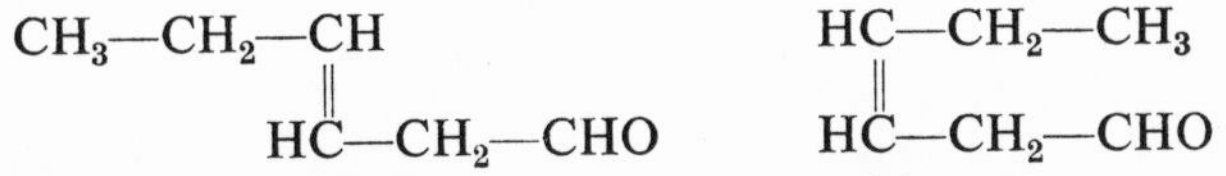

$$CH_3—CH_2—CH \atop \underset{\text{'trans'}}{H\overset{\|}{C}—CH_2—CHO} \qquad\qquad H\overset{\|}{C}—CH_2—CH_3 \atop \underset{\text{'cis'}}{H\overset{\|}{C}—CH_2—CHO}$$

They describe the 'cis' compound as having a 'green odour, fresh and rather natural' and quite different from the 'trans' compound. Both odours are in turn different from the compounds in which the double bond is moved along one place in the chain:

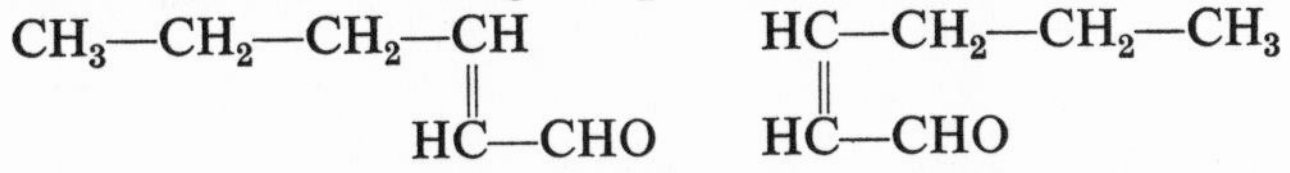

$$CH_3—CH_2—CH_2—CH \atop H\overset{\|}{C}—CHO \qquad\qquad H\overset{\|}{C}—CH_2—CH_2—CH_3 \atop H\overset{\|}{C}—CHO$$

All these examples are no more than 'grab samples' from an immense amount of technical work. They illustrate the fact that odours do not seem to correlate with chemical structure, but as examples they are neither full enough nor systematic enough to show just how vexatious a problem we have here.

Some years ago, G. M. Dyson made a systematic study of a family of compounds known as the 'phenyl mustard oils' that is in many ways a model of how these problems should be tackled. (The only way it could have been improved would have been by using a jury to evaluate the smells. It is possible that he did use one, but he did not say so explicitly in his published papers.)

A substance called 'mustard oil' or allyl isothiocyanate,

$$CH_2{=}CH—CH_2{-}N{=}C{=}S$$

can be isolated from mustard seeds, and has much of the characteristic smell and pungency of mustard. 'Phenyl mustard oil' is a purely synthetic compound with a somewhat similar odour, having the structure:

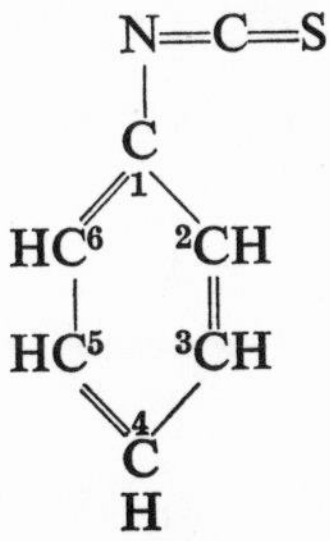

Dyson began by preparing a series of compounds based on the phenyl mustard oil structure, but with one additional group attached to the ring

NCS / C / HC — C—CH₃ / HC — CH / CH
(like phenyl mustard oil but sweeter)

NCS / C / HC — C—Cl / HC — CH / CH
(much like phenyl mustard oil)

NCS / C / HC — C—Br / HC — CH / CH
(less pungent —like anise)

NCS / C / HC — C—I / HC — CH / CH
(sweet odour— like anise)

NCS / C / HC — C—OCH₃ / HC — CH / CH
(harsh pungent odour)

NCS / C / HC — CH / HC — C—CH₃ / CH
(more pungent than phenyl mustard oil)

NCS / C / HC — CH / HC — C—Cl / CH
(very pungent)

NCS / C / HC — CH / HC — C—Br / CH
(slightly pungent)

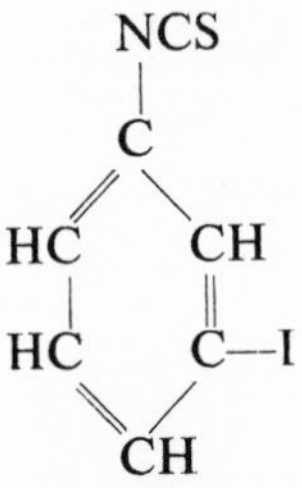

(very slightly pungent, anise type odour)

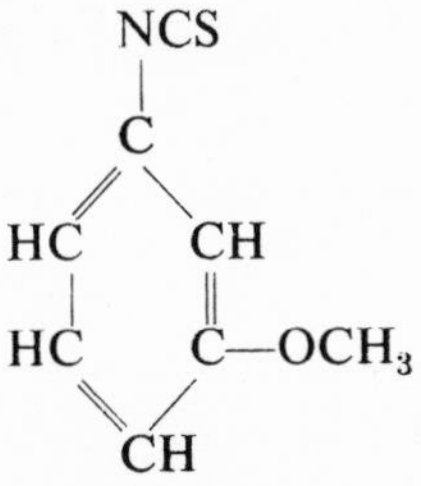

(harsh pungent odour)

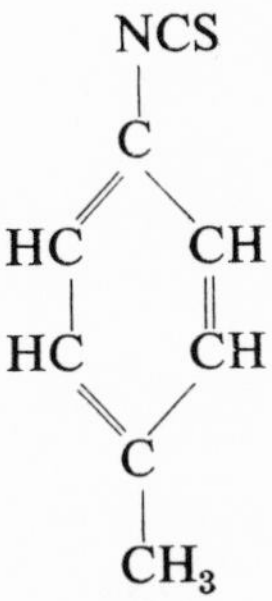

(not pungent, anise odour)

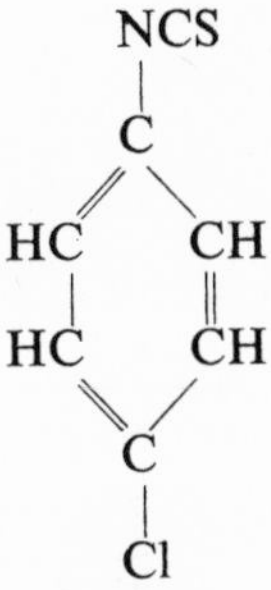

(anise odour, very faintly pungent)

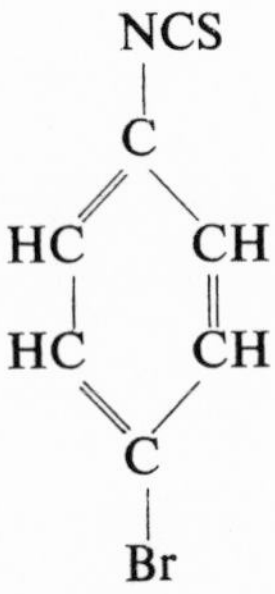

(anise odour)

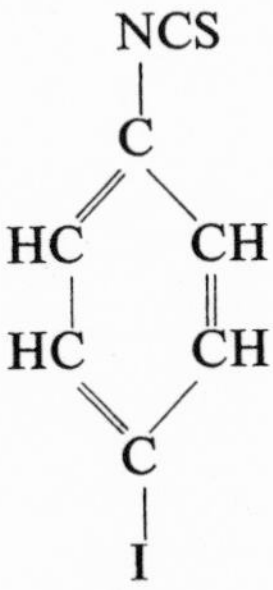

(very sweet anise odour)

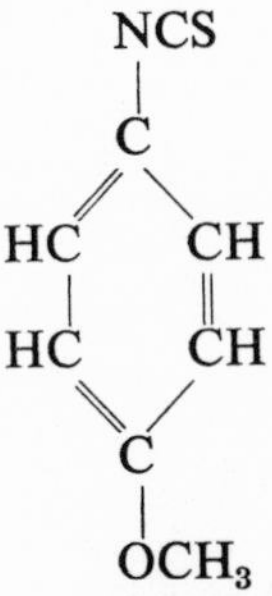

(pronounced anise odour, very soft and delicate)

111

From these results, Dyson concluded that while the basic odour of the phenyl mustard oil was pungent, a substituent in the '2' position (next to the thiocyanate group) tended to make the smell sweeter so as to produce a somewhat floral character, and that it did not matter very much what the extra group was. A substituent in the '3' position tended to enhance the pungency, and one in the '4' position tended to destroy the pungency and replace it with an odour like anise.

He then tried the effect of adding two groups to the basic phenyl mustard oil structure, and found that these rules still held good. For example,

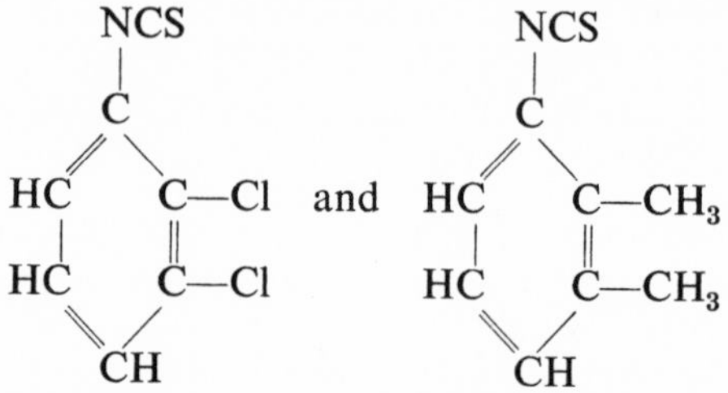

are both pungent, but sweeter than phenyl mustard oil itself because of the modifying effect of the group in the '2' position.

The following compounds show especially interesting additive effects:

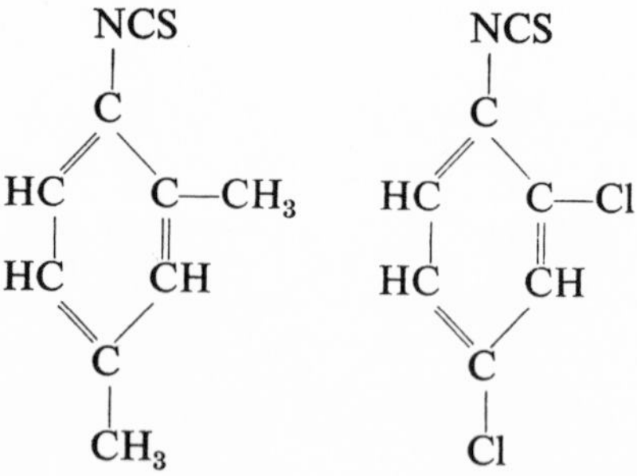

(rather delicate anise)

(sweet anise odour)

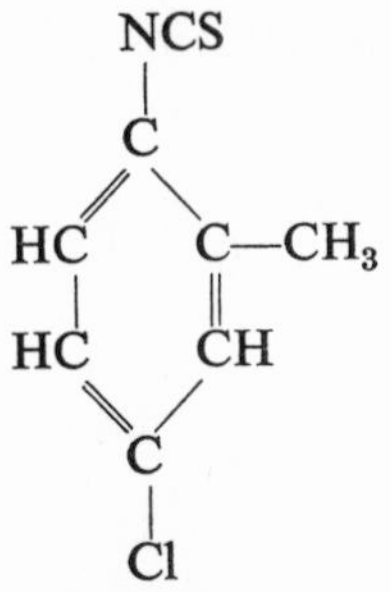

(distinct
anise
odour)

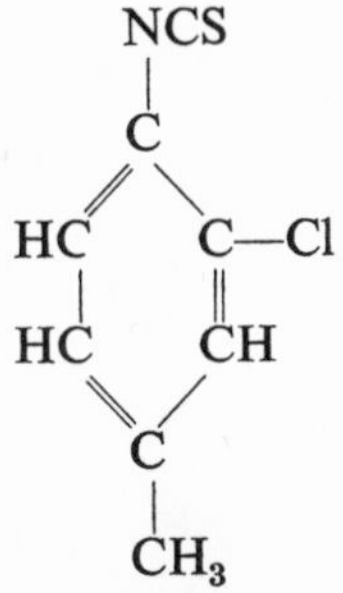

(delicate
spiraea
odour)

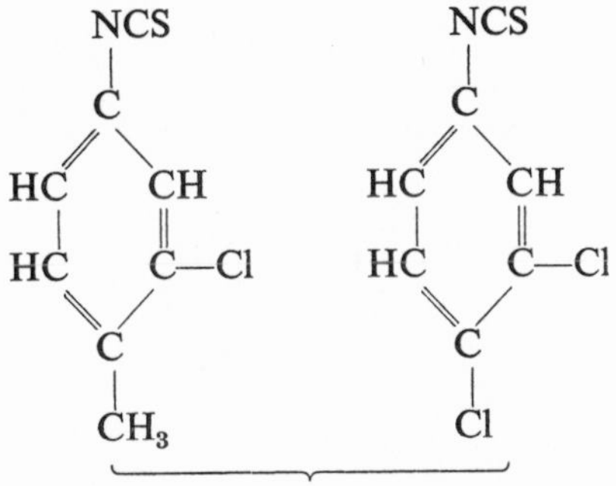

(anise, but noticeably pungent)

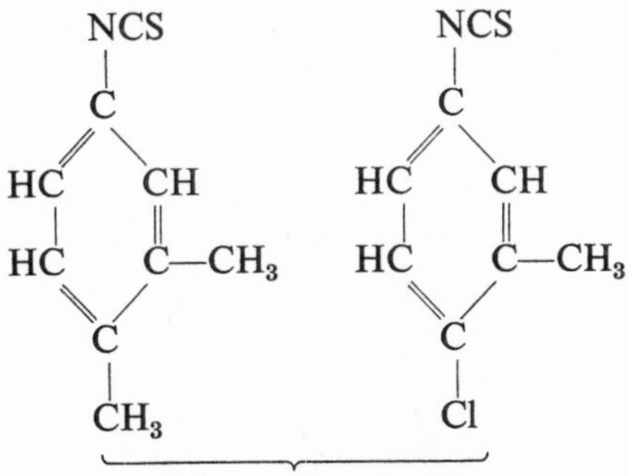

(anise, but less pungent)

The general result of these observations is to confirm the previous generalizations, and to add a rider that the effect of Cl is dominant

113

over that of —CH_3. In fact, the matter of dominance can be carried farther:

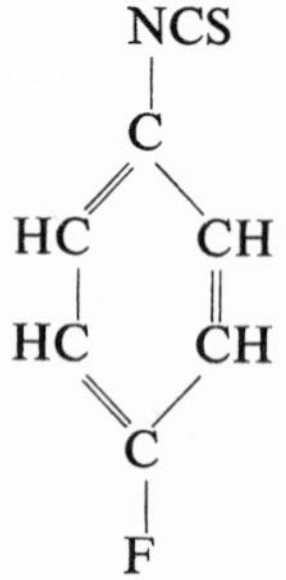

$$
\begin{array}{ccc}
\text{NCS} & \text{NCS} & \text{NCS} \\
| & | & | \\
\text{C} & \text{C} & \text{C} \\
\end{array}
$$

(mainly
mustard
oil, only
slightly
anise)

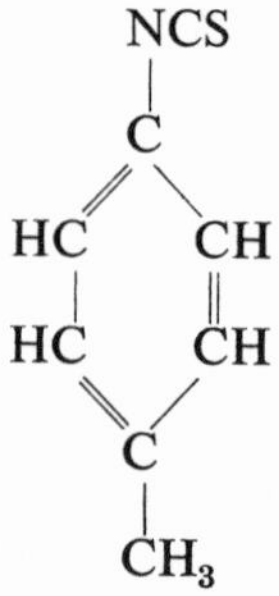

(more
anise
than
pungent)

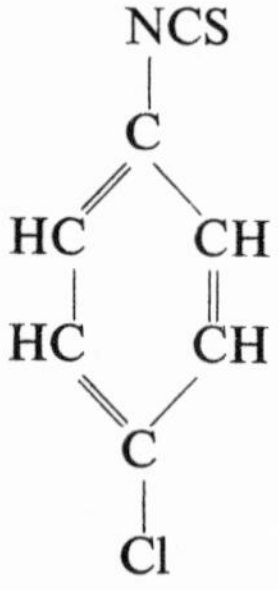

(anise,
very
faintly
pungent)

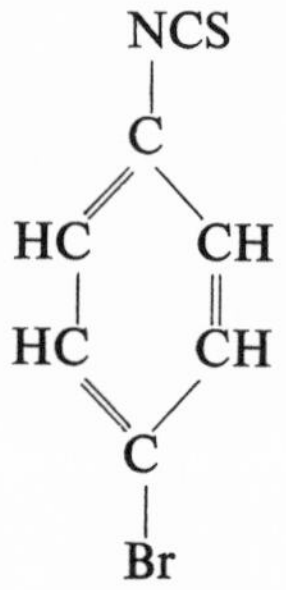

(anise)

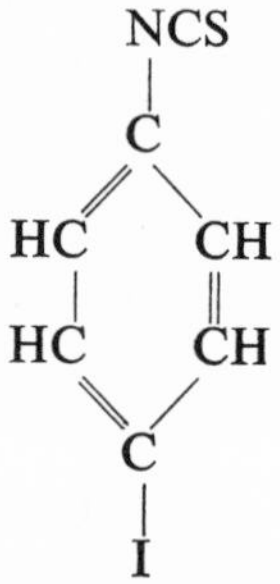

(very sweet
anise-type
odour)

These conclusions are fairly general, for besides the substituents I have shown in the various formulae given above, Dyson got the anise-type of odour with —CN, —OCH$_3$, —O—CH$_2$—CH$_3$, provided they were in the '4' position. But there were limits:

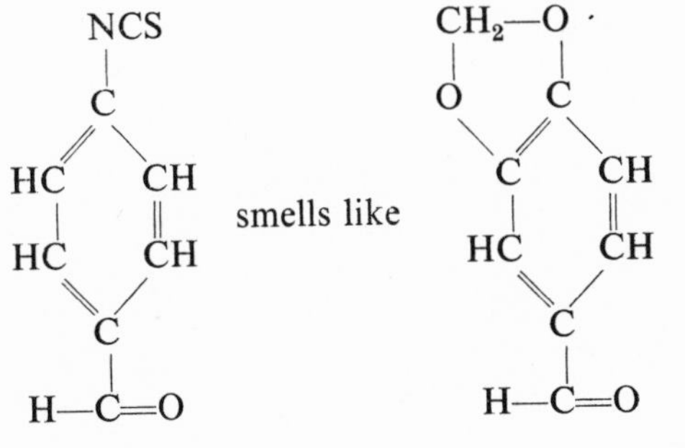

smells like

which is heliotropine!

The regularities that can be observed in this group are unusually systematic for work of this kind, but even so, they have very little transfer value to other groups or families of compounds. For example, benzaldehyde,

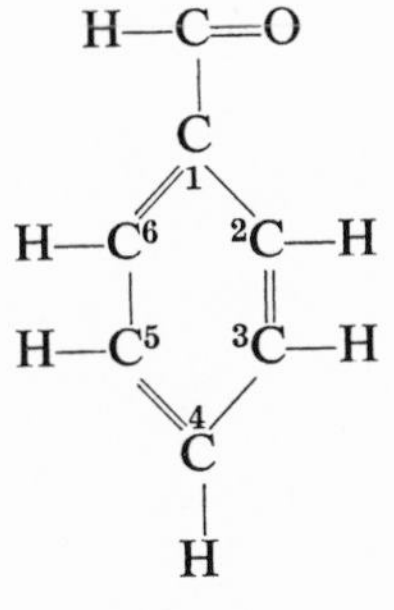

has an almond-like smell, but it does not seem to be modified in the same systematic way by additional groups attached to the ring (though I do not know that any chemist has attacked it as systematically or as comprehensively as Dyson investigated the phenyl mustard oils). About the only generally valid thing one can say is that with benzene derivatives, a new group attached in position '4' (relative to some group already present) is likely to change the character of the smell more than if it is attached in the '2' or '3' position.

If odour does not correlate with the presence of particular atoms or groups of atoms in the molecule, will it correlate with the general chemical reactivity?

In the mustard oils, the isothiocyanate group (—N=C=S) is the most reactive part of the molecule. It reacts rather easily with an alcohol, for example, like this:

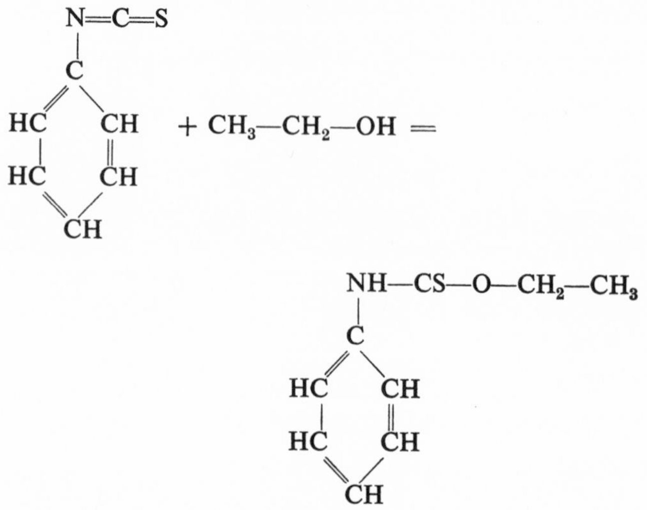

$$N=C=S$$

$$HC \quad CH \quad + CH_3—CH_2—OH =$$
$$HC \quad CH$$
$$CH$$

$$NH—CS—O—CH_2—CH_3$$

$$HC \quad CH$$
$$HC \quad CH$$
$$CH$$

Dyson measured the rate of this reaction when it was undergone by the various phenyl mustard oil derivatives he had prepared in the hope that it would show some correlation with the odour—and he met with no success at all. Some substances with the pungent odour reacted quickly and others very slowly, and the same thing was true of compounds with the anise odour.

At the end, Dyson summed it all up in one crisp sentence: 'It is clear from the work that has been described in these articles, that no chemical data, either from the viewpoint of reactivity or chemical structure will give us the key to the rational, quantitative interpretation of odour phenomena.'

That was more than thirty years ago and it still stands.

Dyson's work was essentially divergent, in the sense that he started with a single basic molecular type and found out whether and how its odour changed when he did something to alter its structure. Other experiments have been convergent, in that a single odour type has been selected and approached from several different chemical directions. The musk odour has been very extensively studied in this way, and molecules of at least five distinct chemical types have been found to possess it.

Natural musk is a substance of animal origin which contains as its

116

active component a substance, muscone, which has the following structure:

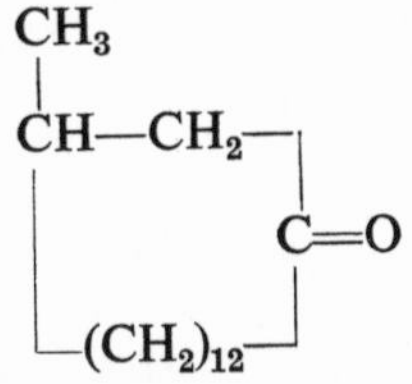

$$
\begin{array}{l}
CH_3 \\
| \\
CH{-}CH_2{-}\!\rceil \\
|\qquad\quad C{=}O \\
|\qquad\quad | \\
\rfloor{-}(CH_2)_{12}{-}\!\rfloor
\end{array}
$$

The molecule has a closed loop or 'ring' or fifteen atoms, and belongs to a class of 'macrocyclic' or 'large ring' compounds. Many other macrocyclic compounds have the musk odour, including exaltolide (mentioned on page 94) and civetone:

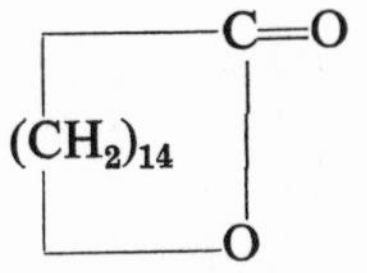

$$
\begin{array}{ll}
\overline{\quad}\;C{=}O & CH{-}(CH_2)_7\!\diagdown \\
(CH_2)_{14}\quad| & \qquad\qquad\quad C{=}O \\
\rule{0pt}{1em}|\qquad\; O & CH{-}(CH_2)_7\!\diagup
\end{array}
$$

Exaltolide 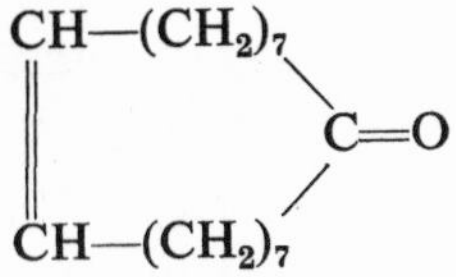   Civetone

In general, a macrocyclic compound with fourteen to nineteen atoms in the ring is likely to have a musk-like odour provided it has one 'functional group' such as $-CO-$, or $-O-CO-$, or $-CO-O-CO-$, as well. A second such group somewhere else in the ring will weaken or destroy the odour, so that this compound, for example, does not have the musk odour:

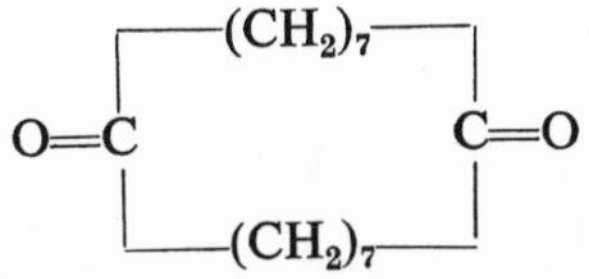

$$
\begin{array}{l}
\overline{\quad}\;(CH_2)_7\;\overline{\quad} \\
O{=}C\qquad\qquad C{=}O \\
\rfloor\;(CH_2)_7\;\rfloor
\end{array}
$$

A great many macrocyclic musks have been synthesized. Their odours are by no means identical either in strength or quality, but they are similar enough to be described as musk-like, and some of them find important applications in perfumery.

Another and rather different group is the sterol musks, first described by Ruzicka and Prelog. Sterols are a biochemically important group of substances which involve a complex system of 'fused'

117

rings. Several vitamins and hormones are related to the sterols. This sterol has a musk odour:

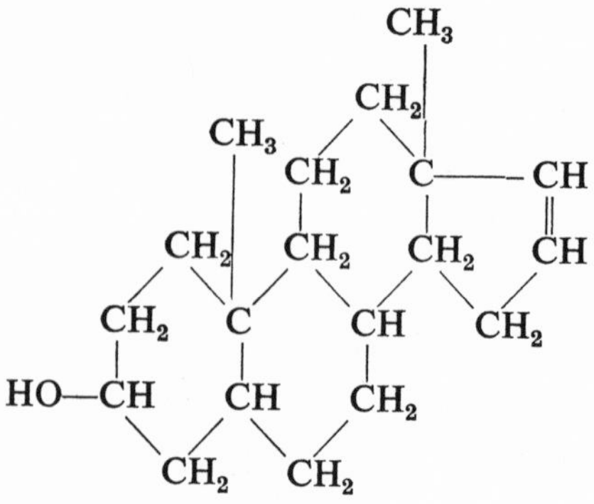

$$
\begin{array}{c}
CH_3 \\
CH_2 \\
CH_3 \quad CH_2 \quad C \text{——} CH \\
CH_2 \quad CH_2 \quad CH_2 \quad \overset{\|}{CH} \\
CH_2 \quad C \quad CH \quad CH_2 \\
HO\text{—}CH \quad CH \quad CH_2 \\
CH_2 \quad CH_2
\end{array}
$$

There are other sterols with this general structure but only a few of them have the musk odour, and it is very sensitive to small changes in the structure.

If the internal cross-linkings that make the sterol a system of fused rings are done away with, and if one or two other changes are made, you get this structure:

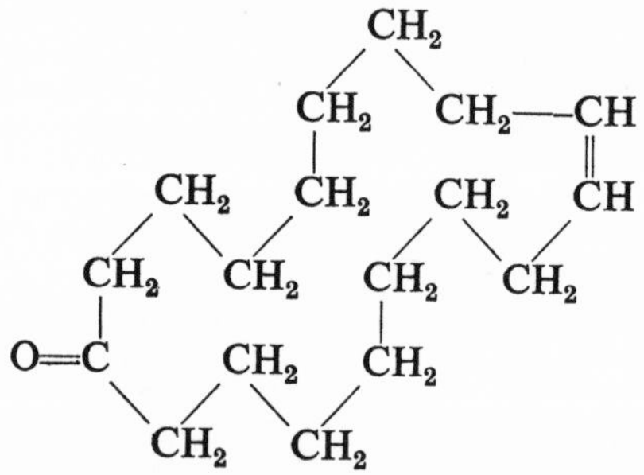

$$
\begin{array}{c}
CH_2 \\
CH_2 \quad CH_2\text{——}CH \\
CH_2 \quad CH_2 \quad CH_2 \quad \overset{\|}{CH} \\
CH_2 \quad CH_2 \quad CH_2 \quad CH_2 \\
O\text{=}C \quad CH_2 \quad CH_2 \\
CH_2 \quad CH_2
\end{array}
$$

If you will count up the —CH_2— groups, you will find that this is the macrocyclic musk, civetone. This may be no more than a remarkable coincidence, but it is probably more than that, because the following compound, in which one of the internal cross-links is present, also has a musk-like odour:

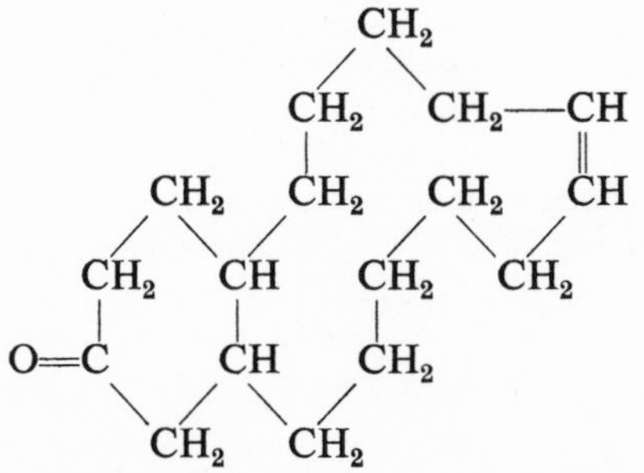

Another, and quite different group is the technically important family of 'nitro musks' of which the following are some typical examples:

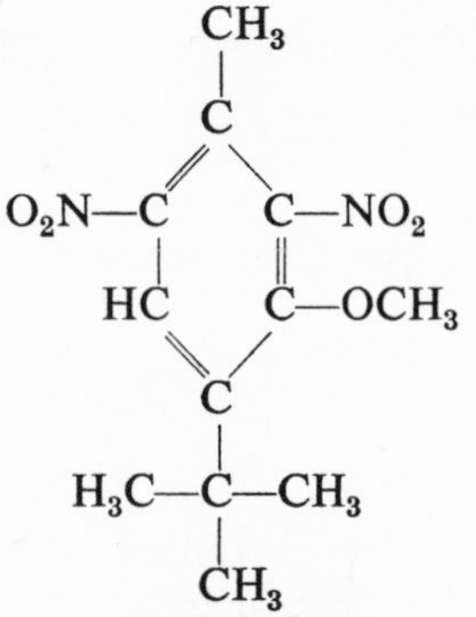

Musk Ambrette

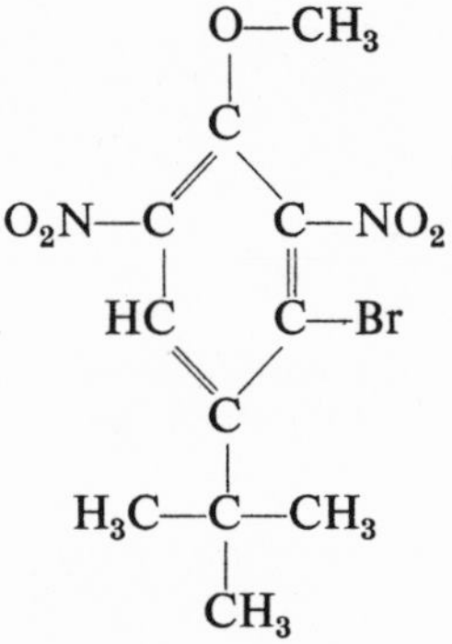

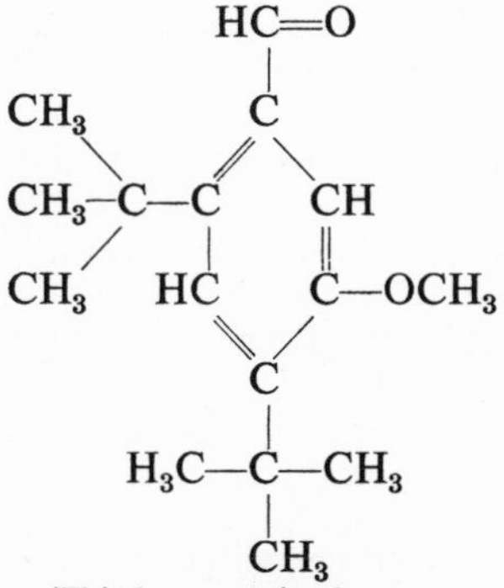

(This has no 'nitro' group,
but it clearly belongs in the
same class)

In addition to these definitely established families of substances which have a musk-like odour but little else in common, there are scattered, passing references in the technical journals to yet other types of substances possessing it to some degree. Evidently, whatever it is that gives rise to a musk odour is not something that is tied to any one type of chemical molecule, or to one kind of chemical reactivity, and equally it is something that can be achieved in a great many different ways. We will consider some of them in later chapters. For the moment, it is sufficient to repeat Dyson's conclusion that chemical structures and activities cannot be made the key to an understanding of odour phenomena.

REFERENCES

M. G. J. BEETS. 'Structure and Odour', in 'Molecular Structure and Organoleptic Quality'. S.C.I. Monograph No. 1, Society of Chemical Industry, London, 1957. pp. 54–90. (Includes an excellent review of the musk chemicals.)

J. V. BRAUN, H. KRÖPER, and H. WIENHAUS. (Odour and Constitution. I.) *Ber.*, **62B,** 2880–2885, 1929.

G. M. DYSON. 'Influence of Chemical Constitution on the Odour of the Mustard Oils', *Perf. Essent. Oil Record,* **17,** 20–22, 1926.

G. M. DYSON. 'Odour and Constitution among the Mustard Oils. I. The Influence of Alkyl Groups', *Perf. Essent. Oil Record,* **19,** 3–5, 1928.

G. M. DYSON. 'Odour and Constitution among the Mustard Oils. II. The Effect of Halogen Substituents', *Perf. Essent. Oil Record,* **19,** 88–91, 1928.

G. M. DYSON. 'Odour and Constitution among the Mustard Oils. III. The Joint Influence of Halogen, Methyl and Nitro Groups', *Perf. Essent. Oil Record,* **19,** 171–174, 1928.

G. M. DYSON. 'Odour and Constitution among the Mustard Oils. IV. The Effect of Fluorine Substitution', *Perf. Essent. Oil Record,* **19,** 341–342, 1928.

G. M. DYSON. 'Odour and Constitution among the Mustard Oils. V. Blending of Mustard Oils', *Perf. Essent. Oil Record,* **20,** 3–5, 1929.

G. M. DYSON. 'Odour and Constitution among the Mustard Oils. VI. Natural Mustard Oils', *Perf. Essent. Oil Record,* **20,** 42–44, 1929.

G. M. DYSON. 'Odour and Constitution among the Mustard Oils. VII. Reactivity and Odour'. *Perf. Essent. Oil Record,* **22,** 278–281, 1931.

V. PRELOG and L. RUZICKA. (Two Steroids from Swine Testes which have a Musk-like Odour.) *Helv. Chim. Acta,* **27,** 61–66, 1944.

T. F. WEST, J. J. STRAUSZ, and D. H. R. BARTON. *Synthetic Perfumes. Their Chemistry and Preparation.* Edward Arnold, London, 1949.

M. WINTER and F. GAUTSCHI. (Odour and Constitution. XX. Synthesis of cis- and trans-3-Hexenal.) *Helv. Chim. Acta,* **45** (7), 2567–2575, 1962.

15

Left and Right

ORGANIC chemical structure theory provides a detailed and comprehensive solution to what would otherwise be a very troublesome fact. There are substances which are perfectly distinct chemically and in other ways too, yet which are made up of molecules containing the same number and the same kind of atoms. They have the same formula but they are not the same substance. They are called isomers of each other.

One of the earliest examples of this to be clearly recognized was a pair of substances, one, ammonium cyanate, was regarded as inorganic from the method of its preparation (from silver cyanate and ammonium chloride), and the other, urea, was classed as an organic substance because it was a waste product of animal metabolism. Both had the formula CH_4N_2O, but their solubilities, crystal forms, and other properties were different. They were 'isomeric', and this was one of the first known examples of isomerism. (These two substances are famous in another way, too, because in 1828 when Wohler found out how to change ammonium cyanate into urea, it was the first time an organic compound had been made from inorganic starting materials without passing them through a living body —but that is another story.)

Without structure theory, the existence of isomers would make chemistry a much more difficult subject than it already is. With structure theory, the following two substances are easily accounted for like this:

$$\text{'Ammonium Cyanate'} \qquad \begin{array}{c} \text{H} \;\; \text{H} \\ \diagdown \!\! \mid \\ \text{N---O---C} \!\equiv\! \text{N} \\ \diagup \!\! \mid \\ \text{H} \;\; \text{H} \end{array} \qquad \text{'Urea'} \qquad \begin{array}{c} \text{H---N---H} \\ \mid \\ \text{C} \!=\! \text{O} \\ \mid \\ \text{H---N---H} \end{array}$$

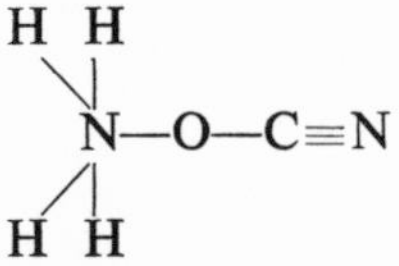

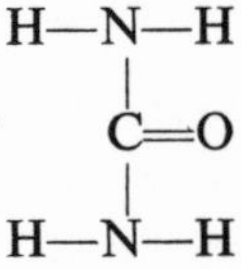

The basic structure theory of Kekulé, with a few simple extensions, can account for every known case of isomerism.

We have already seen examples of two ways isomerism can come about. One is structural or position isomerism, shown, for example, in the phenyl mustard oils that Dyson studied, where a substituent group might be in the 2, 3, or 4, position with respect to the isothio-cyanate group. A second kind of isomerism is 'cis-trans' isomerism, which arises when rigidities (imposed by double bonds or ring struc-tures) make it possible to link the same atoms to the same atoms and in the same order, but with different arrangements in space. Because the difference is spatial, cis-trans isomerism is a kind of stereo-isomerism.

However, it is not the only kind of stereoisomerism.

There is another kind, a kind that is more subtle, more common, and much more important. It was discovered by Louis Pasteur a hundred years ago, and was soon given a structural interpretation by Van't Hoff and Le Bel independently.

This third kind of isomerism is called 'optical isomerism' because in the simplest cases it reveals itself only through a subtle difference in the optical properties of the two isomers. Apart from the optical difference, they are otherwise indistinguishable in nearly every respect.

Optical isomerism can appear in any compound where there is one carbon atom with four different kinds of atoms or groups of atoms attached to it. If the four valences of the carbon atom are directed outwards in space so as to make equal angles with each other, then there are two different ways of attaching four different things to them. It takes a picture or, better still, models to see this properly, but Van't Hoff and Le Bel did see it, and they saw, too, that optical isomers always do have at least one such carbon atom in them.

When four different things are linked to one carbon atom, the two possible forms are related to each other in the same way that a left and a right hand are related. The parts are the same, the structure is the same, and they can do the same things, but they are not exactly the same because one cannot be laid on top of the other so as to coincide point for point. They cannot be superimposed because they are asymmetric. A carbon atom with four different things attached to it is an 'asymmetric carbon atom' and a molecule which contains such a carbon atom can exist in two 'mirror image' forms.

For most chemical purposes, the asymmetry does not matter. A left hand can do everything a right hand can do—with one vital exception. A left hand will not go into a right glove.

Similarly, a left-handed molecule will do everything that its right-handed twin (or enantiomorph) will do—until it is asked to react with another asymmetric molecule. When that happens there is a difference between the way 'right-handed-A' reacts with 'right-handed-B' and the way it reacts with 'left-handed-B'.

Since most biological substances are very complex structurally, there are innumerable opportunities for this kind of isomerism to occur, and the interesting and significant fact is that living things always produce and use only one of the two possible forms. What is more, all the living things on earth, from the most insignificant scrap of moss to the largest elephant, all have the same kind of 'handedness'. Life as we know it in all its diversity, fits into a common symmetry pattern, presumably because it has all evolved from a single primordial prototype. (One of the most eagerly awaited results of a trip to Mars is an observation of the molecular symmetry of whatever life is found there. If it is opposite to ours it must have had an independent beginning. If it is the same as ours it could be coincidence, or it could mean that our life and theirs had a common origin.)

The fact that all terrestrial life belongs to one of two possible forms which differ only in their molecular symmetry, means that the proteins and carbohydrates in our bodies and our diets could exist in a through-the-looking-glass form that would be the same as ours in all the non-essential ways, but which would be utterly alien, useless, indigestible, and completely unassimilable by any living thing in our world. Chemists have synthesized mixtures of equal parts of the left- and right-handed forms of a nutrient substance, and have fed the mixture to some living thing, most often to a yeast or other microbe. They find that the form that is 'natural' (here on earth) is utilized or metabolized, and the other form remains untouched. The reactions that go on in living things are guided and controlled by enzymes, which are highly complex organic substances with the properties of catalysts. Enzymes are themselves asymmetric, and they impress their asymmetry on the reactions they govern and the products they make.

They are stereospecific.

Now what has all this to do with smells and smelling?

First, it poses the obvious question: do substances which are optical isomers—which differ only in their symmetry—have the same smell?

At present, the best answer to this is—'pretty nearly'.

There are several known pairs of optical isomers whose threshold concentration and odour quality are indistinguishable; there are several other pairs which were at one time thought to be different but which became indistinguishable when they were sufficiently purified; and there are a few pairs which have still not been shown to have exactly the same smell even after careful purification, though the difference is rather small—more a matter of 'note' than of 'character'.

123

It is possible that these residual differences are real, but they could also be due to traces of impurities.

For example, the threshold concentration of one substance might be 1 part in 10^6 of air. If it was contaminated with 0·01 per cent of an impurity, and if the threshold of the impurity was 1 part in 10^{12} of air, at a low enough concentration of the mixture it would be the impurity that was smelled rather than the main substance, notwithstanding the fact that the main substance was 99·99 per cent pure. Not many chemicals are that pure.

In at least one of the reported cases there is another explanation. Doll and Bournot purified the left- and right-handed forms of menthol very carefully, and found that they had the same minimum stimulus and the same odour up to twenty times the threshold concentration, after which they diverged. But menthol is not a simple odorant, for it stimulates the cold receptors also, and according to Hensel and Zotterman this probably does involve an enzymatic mechanism. The combined sensation of smell and cooling therefore should be different for the two forms of menthol.

So it comes to this: optical isomers when pure have the same or nearly the same *odours*. There are no known cases where one of the isomers has an odour and the other has no odour at all. If one isomer smells the other smells also, and the smells are similar if not identical.

From this we can draw a very important conclusion.

I said a moment ago that the chemical activities of enzymes are always highly stereospecific. If an enzyme can effect a reaction in the right-handed form of a compound it will not touch the left-handed form, and *vice versa*. The fact that both members of an optically isomeric pair smell—and smell similarly—shows, I think conclusively, that the basic process of olfactory stimulation is not a chemical reaction. The odourous molecules do not oxidize or reduce or otherwise react chemically with the membrane of the olfactory cell, and they are not themselves oxidized or otherwise chemically transformed in the process of stimulating a sensation. Any such reaction would almost certainly require an enzyme to make it go, and as long as enzymes are stereo-specific, the left- and right-handed forms of an odourous substance would behave differently.

There is another kind of interaction between an enzyme and an odourous molecule which has been suggested to account for the phenomena of olfaction, and especially for the very low threshold concentrations of many odours. G. B. Kistiakowski suggested that in the membranes of the olfactory cells there might be a sequence of reactions like this:

$$A \xrightarrow{\text{enzyme a}} B \xrightarrow{\text{enzyme b}} C$$

Normally there would be only a little substance 'B' present because it would be destroyed as fast as it was formed. If an odourous substance somehow interfered with the enzyme 'b', then the concentration of the substance 'B' would rise dramatically, and its concentration would reach a level quite out of proportion to the amount of the odourous substance needed to block the enzyme. (The volume of water that spills out of a bath tub bears no relation to the size of the sponge that blocks the overflow pipe!) Kistiakowski suggested that this was the way the enzymes 'amplified' the weak signal from a small amount of odourous material so as to generate a strong sensation. He thought, too, that the high informational capacity of the olfactory system could be accounted for if there were enough enzyme systems of this sort, each sensitive to a different primary odour.

Unfortunately, this attractive idea is irretrievably wrecked on the intractable fact that optically isomeric pairs of substances both smell, and what is more, both smell much the same. This is plainly inconsistent with the very high stereospecificity of enzymes.

It will not do to say that the odourous substances somehow override the stereospecificity and exercise a generalized effect on the enzyme which is the same for the left- as for the right-handed form. Substances which can do this are well known. Hydrocyanic or prussic acid, HCN, is a good example, and it is a dangerous and deadly poison just because it does have a general and non-specific effect on enzymes. It is poisonous because it throws the whole of our body chemistry into chaos and confusion by indiscriminately blocking all sorts of enzyme-controlled processes.

The situation is therefore clear.

Odourous substances are not usually dangerous poisons and their left- and right-handed forms have similar smells. Therefore, olfaction is not primarily a chemical phenomenon. The failure of Dyson and others to correlate odour with chemical structure or reactivity is no accident.

REFERENCES

W. DOLL and K. BOURNOT. (The Odour of Optical Antipodes.) *Pharmazie*, **4**, 224–227, 1949.

H. HENSEL and Y. ZOTTERMAN. 'The Effect of Menthol on the Thermoreceptors', *Acta Physiol. Scandinavia*, **24**, 27–34, 1951.

G. B. KISTIAKOWSKI. 'On the Theory of Odours', *Science*, **112**, 154–155, 1950.

Y.-R. NAVES. 'The Relationship Between the Stereochemistry and Odourous Properties of Organic Substances', in 'Molecular Structure and Organoleptic Quality'. S.C.I. Monograph No. 1, Society of Chemical Industry, London, 1957. pp. 38–51.

16

Taking Shape

IF the odours of chemical substances are not due to their chemical properties, what are they due to? What other kinds of properties are there?

It is customary to classify the properties of things as either chemical or physical. If we define the properties of a substance as the various ways in which it makes its presence manifest to our senses, we can distinguish between chemical and physical properties like this: the manifestation of chemical properties is accompanied by a change in the chemical composition or constitution, whereas when physical properties are manifested we have no reason to suspect any change in the molecular make-up. To take an extreme example, when dynamite explodes the change is chemical, and when a steam boiler bursts the change is physical. In other cases it may be difficult to decide whether a change is one or the other, simply because the changes in molecular make-up may be too subtle to be detected by the techniques we have. This bothers people who like to make nice tidy classification schemes in their minds and then expect nature to conform to them, but they are overlooking the fact that to describe nature we must first observe her. It is possible for a change to be both chemical and physical, and it can also be neither, but something else, radioactive, perhaps.

However, these are rather fine points, and for the moment we can think of physical properties as involving things like magnetism, electric polarity, the ability to absorb light, and so on.

Correlations of odour with all these and with many others have been sought and now and then claimed, but so far without any real success. They have been well reviewed down to about 1950 by R. W. Moncrieff in his very thorough book on taste and smell, and the theories associated with these correlations have been critically appraised by Jones and Jones in a paper that appeared at about the same time as Moncrieff's book. What they all boiled down to was the fact that if smell was not a chemical phenomenon, there did not seem to be a good physical explanation of it either. Since 1950 there has been a little progress which I will try to describe.

First, however, I must say something about a theory which

enjoyed a brief vogue after 1947 and is now discarded, but which was still given as current in the 1962 edition of a well-known encyclopaedia.

In 1947, Beck and Miles suggested that various odourous molecules could absorb certain infrared radiations more or less strongly, and if the olfactory nerve cells could radiate these wavelengths the cells would be preferentially cooled when odorous molecules with the right absorbing properties came near them, and this cooling would be registered as a smell sensation. They described some experiments with honey bees in the vicinity of infrared-transmitting windows that appeared to bear this out.

Both the theory and the experiments have been called in question. For the theory to be sound, the nerve cells *must* be warmer or cooler than the surrounding air, because if the air and the cells are at the same temperature then no change in the composition of the air can change the temperature of the cells. Therefore, on their theory, olfactory sensations ought to stop when the air is at the same temperature as the nose—and of course they do not disappear. There are other objections too. Even with a temperature gradient to enable the odourous molecules to effect some preferential cooling, the 'signal' from their specific effect would (at low concentrations) be indistinguishable from the non-specific cooling by the very numerous molecules of oxygen and nitrogen in the air. With this theory the very low thresholds of many substances would be inexplicable. Finally, the insect experiments were repeated by J. W. Johnston with some added precautions, and the results were negative. For all these reasons, the theory of Beck and Miles has not won general acceptance.

Another possibility was looked at by Mullins, who wondered whether the effect of odourous molecules on olfactory cells might be something like the way narcotics and anaesthetics act on nerves—but again the results were not very convincing.

At the present time there are two main theories in the field, neither especially new, but both wearing new dresses.

The first seeks to relate the odourous properties of molecules to their shape, and hence to their ability to fill appropriate sites on the surface of the olfactory cells, and so it may be called a 'site filling' theory. We have already touched the edge of it in Chapter 13 when considering the ideas of Davies and Taylor.

To calculate the threshold concentration, they assumed that the ability of the molecule to 'puncture' the olfactory membrane depended on a combination of affinity plus efficacy, the one determining the concentration of odourous molecules in the surface layer, and the other being related to the cross-sectional area of the molecule.

Both these properties would depend in a rather general way on the shape and chemical make-up of the molecule. M. G. J. Beets has refined their ideas so as to account for the variety of odours, but without trying to follow up their quantitative estimation of the threshold concentrations.

To explain why there are so many odours, Beets introduced an idea which he called the 'profile-functional-group' or PFG concept. By this he meant that the shape or profile which an irregular lump of a molecule presents to the olfactory membrane depends on the location in the molecule of the functional group that ties it to the membrane. The functional group also helps to determine the affinity. (A functional group is a sub-assembly of atoms which is not usually capable of separate existence but whose presence as part of a molecule confers certain well-defined properties or functions on that molecule. The alcohol, aldehyde, and isothiocyanate groups,

$$\text{C—OH,} \quad \text{—}\overset{\displaystyle \overset{O}{\|}}{C}\text{—H,} \quad \text{and} \quad \text{—N}{=}\text{C}{=}\text{S, are examples.})$$

Evidently, on this theory, both the affinity and the efficacy determine the physiological activity, and they are related to both the chemical properties (the functional groups) and the physical shape or profile of the molecule.

For example, in the phenyl mustard oils which Dyson studied, the functional group that is supposed to tie the molecule down to the membrane is the —N=C=S group, but the position of the second group alters the profile and hence the kind of site the molecule attaches itself to. This explains why the position of the second group is usually more important than its identity in determining the type of the odour. If there are two (or more) functional groups capable of tying the molecule to the membrane in different ways or different places, the result will be that some are tied one way and some another, giving a complex odour.

The basic assumption that the profile determines the kind of site and the functional group the affinity of the molecule for the site, is considered to be too restrictive, and the site selection is thought to be determined by both the functional group and the profile. In the mustard oil family, most substituents in the '4' position with respect to the —NCS group give an anise odour; but if the substituent is an aldehyde group the odour is completely altered to heliotrope (page 115). This would be explained by supposing that as a functional group the aldehyde is dominant over the isothiocyanate and carries most of the molecules into a different kind of site. Here the effect of the functional group plays the major role.

128

Beets suggests that the opposite can also be true, and points to these three substances as all having a similar bitter-almond odour because they fit into one kind of site:

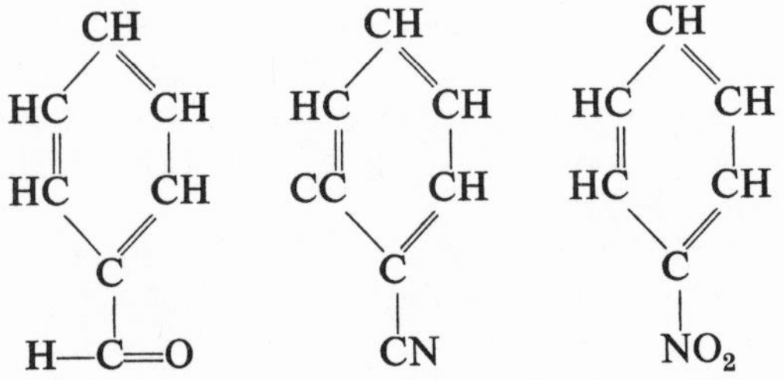

If the profile is changed, the molecules no longer fit that site and the odour is changed to vanilla in these three compounds:

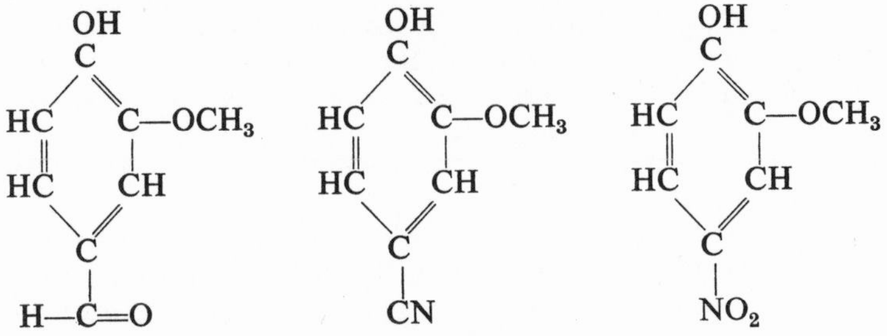

Here the profile is dominant over the functional group.

Thus the interplay between the molecular shape and a functional group provides a facile explanation of many puzzling things. Indeed, Beets' theory is almost too facile. It explains all the things one knows already, but it has very little power to predict things that are still unknown. This does not mean that it is wrong—but it is clearly not as useful as a theory that can tell us in advance what kind of odour a new compound will have.

As so often happens in science, the same idea was being worked on independently in other places. (Site filling theories are not new, Troland had quite a good one as long ago as 1930.) In 1952, J. E. Amoore took up an idea very similar to Beets' except that it assigns rather more weight to the molecular shape or profile than it does to the functional group. His theory has since been developed in considerable detail and in a sense it goes on from where Beets' theory leaves off.

Amoore started from a suggestion by Moncrieff that the odour of a chemical depends on its molecules being shaped so as to fit more or less accurately into a corresponding socket or site on the receptor organ. If this is so, then all chemicals with similar odours will have similar shapes—or, more precisely, similarly shaped parts. A substance that can fit into only one type of socket will have a primary odour, and the number of primary odours would have to be fairly small because the number of sufficiently distinctive socket shapes is limited. It follows, too, that for the sockets to be distinctive they must be rather inflexible.

There will probably be certain substances that can fit more than one type of site, but on probability grounds they will be a minority. If we took a random collection of molecules, one in ten might happen to fit into any one type of site, and it is an elementary proposition in probability theory that if the chance that 'A' will happen is 1 in 10, and the chance that 'B' will happen is 1 in 10, then the chance of *both* 'A' and 'B' happening is 1 in 100.

Amoore made this the basis for an ingenious method of identifying the primary odours his theory calls for.

If molecules able to fit only one type of site are commoner than molecules capable of fitting into two or three different sites, we would expect to find far more pure substances with the simple, primary odours than with complex odours. (This applies to pure substances, and once we go to mixtures the number of possibilities is much larger.) Amoore went through the chemical literature looking for descriptions of the odours of organic compounds, and made the following list.

Name of odour			Number of compounds
'Camphoraceous'	.	.	106
'Pungent'	.	.	95
'Ethereal'	.	.	53
'Floral'	.	.	71
'Pepperminty'	.	.	77
'Musky'	.	.	69
'Putrid'	.	.	49
'Almond'	.	.	30
'Aromatic'	.	.	27
'Aniseed'	.	.	12
'Lemon'	.	.	7
'Cedar'	.	.	7
'Garlic'	.	.	7
'Rancid'	.	.	6
Total	.	.	616

Taking into account the number of times the various names appeared and the stiffness of the molecular structures, he concluded that the first seven odours on this list are probably primary odours, the last four are complex, and he thought that 'almond', 'aromatic', and 'aniseed' were doubtful and might be either.

The next thing was to see what was known about the shapes of the molecules corresponding to each of these apparently primary odours, so as to verify first of all whether they do have a similarity in shape or profile, and then from this to deduce the probable shapes of the sockets or receptor sites on the olfactory membrane. This was done with models, and the results agreed with the assumption that the first seven odours on the list are primary, and the rest, including the doubtful three, are probably complex.

The seven primary sites were worked out in a preliminary way. The 'ethereal' socket, for example, is supposed to be an elongated trough, 5 Ångstrom units wide by 4 deep, and about 18 Ångstroms long. (1 Ångstrom unit = 10^{-8} cm.) An ethereal smell sensation may require the simultaneous presence of more than one molecule of the odourous substance in the site.

The 'camphoraceous' site is pictured as an elliptical bowl, 4 Å. deep, 9 A. long, and 7·5 Å. wide. The 'musky' receptor site is similar but larger, 9 Å. wide by 11·5 Å. long. The 'floral' receptor site is supposed to have a more complicated shape, consisting of a circular hole, 9 Å. in diameter, with a deeper trough, 4 Å. wide, starting at the middle and running out for a distance of 7·5 Å. beyond the edge of the hole. The remaining sites are somewhat simpler in shape, but call for certain localized chemical affinities to attract certain kinds of functional groups in the odourous molecules. Thus Amoore and Beets have independently converged on the same idea: that the meshing of the odourous molecule and the olfactory membrane depends on both the profile and the functional groups of the odourous substance.

Neither of these theories suggests how the molecules actually generate a nerve impulse by fitting themselves into the appropriate sockets, or how they get themselves out again to make way for the next comer.

The most crucial test of any scientific theory is its ability to make verifiable predictions, and Amoore's theory is unique among the site filling theories in having been worked out in enough detail to be tested in this way. Rubin, Apotheker and Lutmer, for example, estimated in advance the probable shapes of these three molecules:

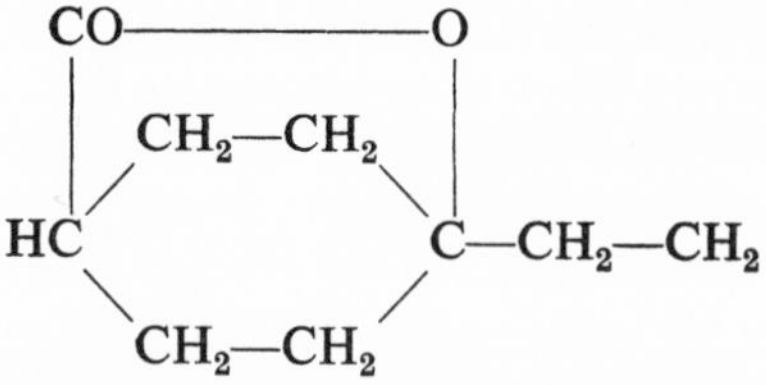

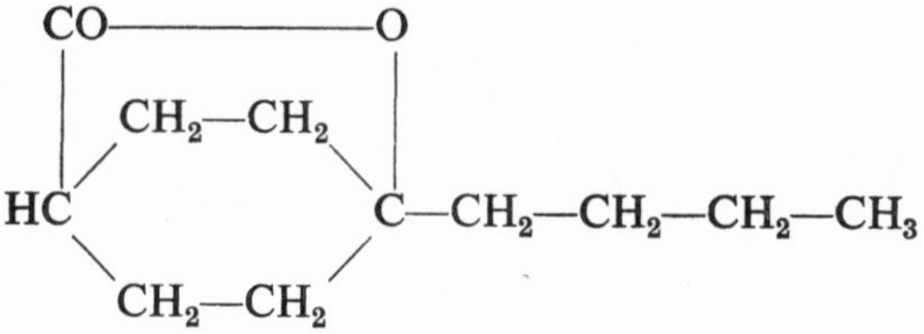

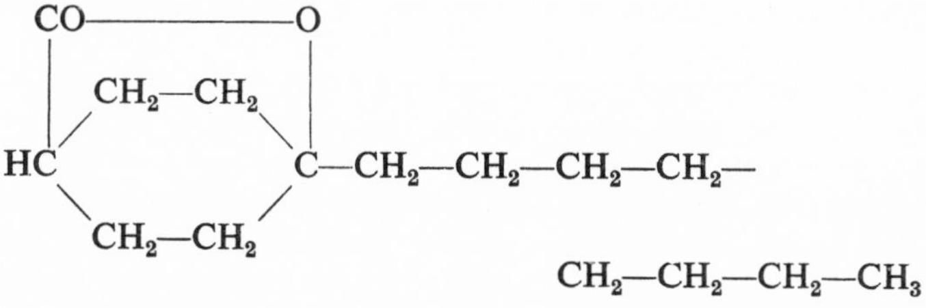

$$CO \text{---} O$$
$$| \quad CH_2 \text{---} CH_2 \quad |$$
$$HC \quad C \text{---} CH_2 \text{---} CH_2$$
$$\quad CH_2 \text{---} CH_2$$

$$CO \text{---} O$$
$$| \quad CH_2 \text{---} CH_2 \quad |$$
$$HC \quad C \text{---} CH_2 \text{---} CH_2 \text{---} CH_2 \text{---} CH_3$$
$$\quad CH_2 \text{---} CH_2$$

$$CO \text{---} O$$
$$| \quad CH_2 \text{---} CH_2 \quad |$$
$$HC \quad C \text{---} CH_2 \text{---} CH_2 \text{---} CH_2 \text{---} CH_2 \text{---}$$
$$\quad CH_2 \text{---} CH_2$$
$$CH_2 \text{---} CH_2 \text{---} CH_2 \text{---} CH_3$$

The first of the three has a rather compact, globular shape, and this and its size should make it fit the 'camphoraceous' site rather well. The third one has a very long 'tail' and should therefore fit the 'floral' site better, while the middle one might be expected to fit both sites and should combine both odours. Several other related compounds with predictable odours were also prepared, and these authors concluded that, 'to a very reasonable degree the characteristics of the odours follow the pattern predicted by Amoore'. Other tests, mainly by J. W. Johnston, have had some success in verifying the predictions of the theory with respect to both the quality and the intensity of the odour.

More recently, Johnston has made a very careful attempt to establish the validity of the basic assumption that there are primary odours and that 'musk' is one of them. This is important because, whether or not the site filling theory is right, an experimentally verified primary odour will always be a useful fixed point to come back to. Using six trained odour judges, Johnston presented various chemically distinct musk perfumes to them under controlled conditions of temperature, humidity, and concentration of the odorous material. He also checked the purity of his chemicals by a very sensitive technique of gas chromatography that has only recently been perfected. The results showed that the six judges could not distinguish reliably between musks belonging to three different chemical classes.

Johnston concluded from this that the musk smell must be stimulated by a single type of receptor organ and is therefore probably primary. This would be consistent with Amoore's theory, but it would not prove the theory correct. A primary odour implies a single, distinctive trigger, but not necessarily a site filling trigger. Before I look at some of the alternatives I must examine Johnston's experiment with the musks and Amoore's general theory a little more closely.

Johnston showed that six judges usually confused the musk odours of three classes of chemicals, but M. Guillot found something very different. He took ten people, apparently at random, and found among them several distinct types of partial anosmia (inability to perceive smells). One woman, for example, could not smell the violet odour of methyl ionone, though she could smell its 'woody' component; and several other people could not perceive the bitter almond odour of hydrocyanic acid. His results with the musk chemicals were especially interesting in the light of Amoore's theory. He located one person who could not smell the musk odour of the sterol shown on page 118, but who could smell other musks perfectly well. Several people could not smell the macrocyclic musks but could smell other kinds, and one person could not smell either the steroid or the macrocyclic musks but could perceive the nitro musks normally. These results were verified for him by J. LeMagnen.

Thus Guillot's conclusion was that there must be several sites capable of registering a musk-like odour, and that some people are deficient in one type but not another. This exactly contradicts Johnston's results. The explanation is probably that Johnston was betrayed by his own carefulness! His six judges were sifted out of a. group of thirty-seven beginners, the selection being based on their all-round reliability in smelling a considerable variety of substances, including various musk chemicals. His criteria of a qualified judge automatically eliminated people with partial anosmias, and Guillot, by contrast, went looking for just such people—and found them.

Both lots of experiments were good and gave good answers, but not to the same question.

Johnston thought he was showing that the musk odour was primary

133

Formula	Odour Test (Man)	Melon Fly Tests	
		Olfactometer	Wick Test
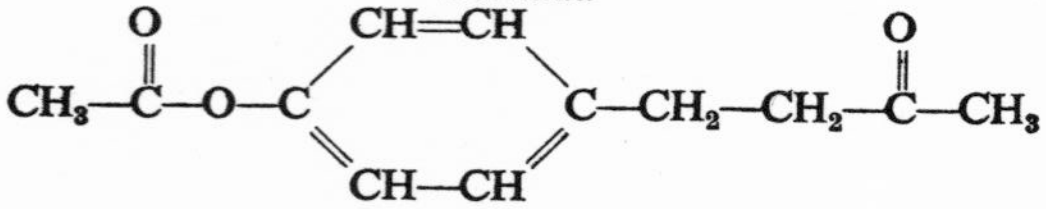	Weak raspberry	34	88
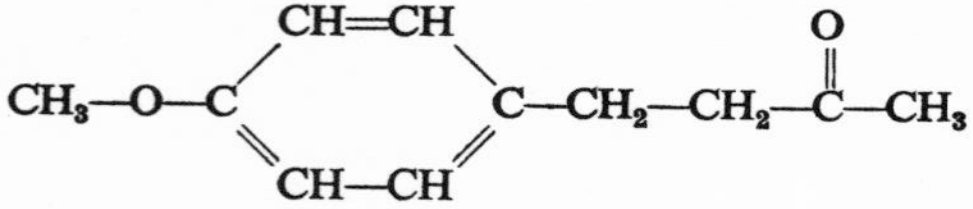	Weak raspberry	33	100 (standard)
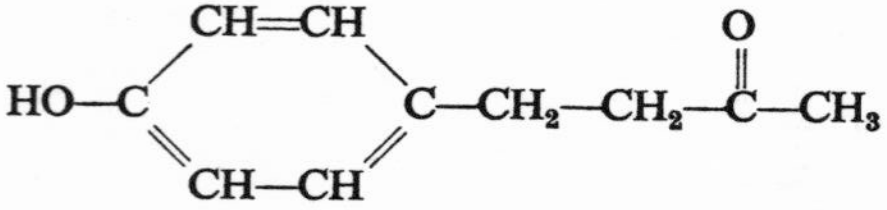	Weak raspberry	20	400
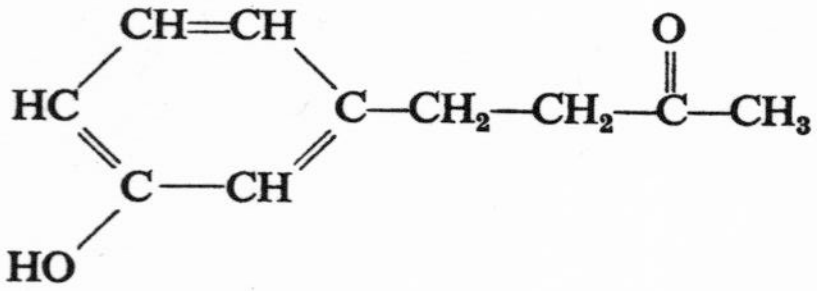	Neither fruity nor raspberry	32	13
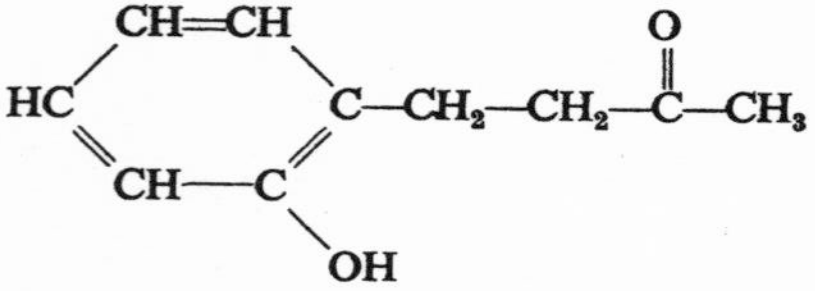	Neither fruity nor raspberry	1	0

134

Structure	Odor		
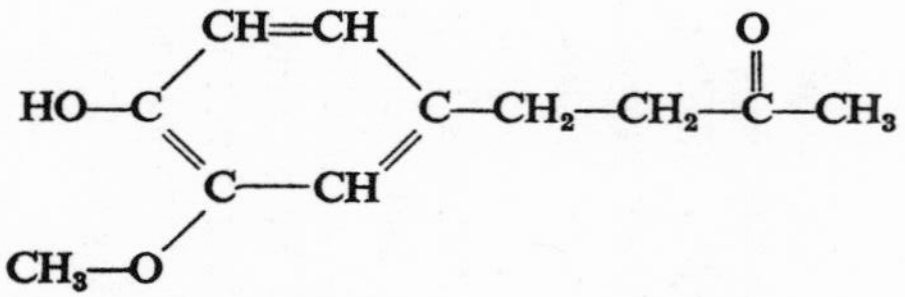 HO—C₆H₃(OCH₃)—CH₂—CH₂—C(=O)—CH₃	Neither fruity nor raspberry	21	50
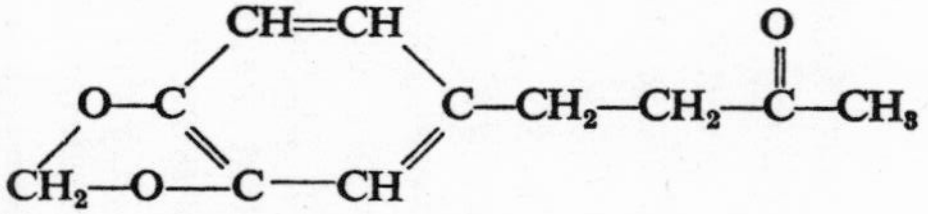 (cyclic OCH₂O)—C₆H₃—CH₂—CH₂—C(=O)—CH₃	Neither fruity nor raspberry	31	Not tested
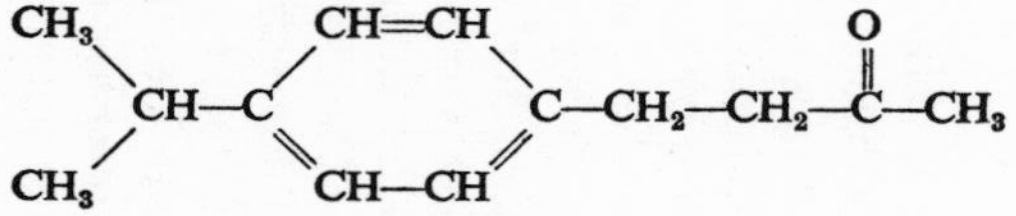 (CH₃)₂CH—O—C₆H₃—CH₂—CH₂—C(=O)—CH₃	Neither fruity nor raspberry	20	0
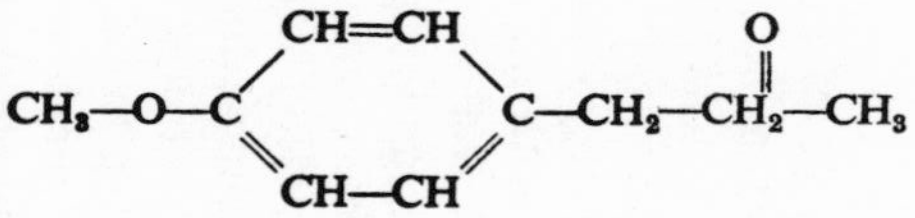 CH₃—O—C₆H₄—CH₂—CH₂—C(=O)—CH₃	Neither fruity nor raspberry	20	0

because people with all-round smelling abilities confuse the various types. Guillot and LeMagnen showed that people who lack this all-round ability may be able to distinguish them. Something similar has been observed with people who are partially colour blind: they can distinguish the colours of objects which are the same to persons with normal sight. Guillot's results cannot be ascribed to impure chemicals, for it was not a matter of more or less subtle differences in quality—people could smell certain smells very well, or they could not smell them at all.

The prevalence and precise details of these partial anosmias needs to be much more carefully studied before any secure conclusions can be drawn, but as things stand, Guillot's work suggests that the musk odour is not a 'primary' in the sense used by Amoore.

I think that in general the existence of partial anosmias and differences in olfactory capability among human beings can be taken as established, and therefore it is interesting to see whether the same phenomenon extends to other creatures.

In Chapter 6, various substances were described which attract melon flies. The type compound was anisyl acetone:

$$CH_3-O-C \underset{\diagdown CH-CH}{\overset{CH=CH \diagup}{\diagup \diagdown}} C-CH_2-CH_2-\overset{\overset{O}{\|}}{C}-CH_3$$

Many variants of this structure were made and tested for melon fly attraction, using two different test methods. One was an 'olfactometer test' in which the flies were given a choice of plain water or water solutions (or emulsions) of three different chemicals and a repellency rating obtained by dividing the number of flies caught by a chemical with the number caught by plain water. The other test was a 'wick test' in which the chemical was absorbed on a cotton 'dental roll' and exposed for several days, and the activity was measured by comparing the number of flies attracted during a 15-minute period with the number attracted by a standard, high-potency chemical lure. The two test methods did not always give consistent measures of the attractiveness, and quantitatively they left something to be desired, but they did show whether or not the insects paid much attention to the chemicals.

In a recent paper, Winter has reported on the odours (as judged by six experienced perfume chemists) of several of these same compounds. The results of these tests and the melon fly attraction tests are brought together in the table on pages 134 and 135.

It seems clear that the ability to attract the insects does not correlate with the smell as perceived by man. If Amoore's theory is correct, this would mean that the insects have a type of site which the man lacks. This is perfectly possible, but it is a slippery assumption to make because the theory loses its point and value if the number of sites we have to assume grows too large.

The phenomena of partial anosmia in men and animals is a serious obstacle to Amoore's theory, and it is by no means the only one. With only seven primary odours (one, 'pungent', possibly not an odour at all a 'pain reaction' sent through a separate nerve system) I think it is impossible to account for the known and very high informational capacity of the olfactory apparatus. In other words, seven primary odours cannot be combined in enough ways to do what we know the nose can do, and therefore, for reasons I have already considered in Chapter 11, I think the number of primaries in man is more likely to be of the order of twenty-five or thirty. Amoore's theory could be stretched to do this, but in doing so it would lose the simplicity which is its principal attraction.

REFERENCES

J. E. AMOORE. 'Stereochemical Specificities of Human Olfactory Receptors', *Perf. Essent. Oil Record*, **43**, 321–323, 330, 1952.

J. E. AMOORE. 'The Stereochemical Theory of Olfaction. 1. Identification of the Seven Primary Odours', *Proc. Sci. Sect., Toilet Goods Assn.*, Special Supplement to No. 37, pp. 1–12, 1962.

J. E. AMOORE. 'The Stereochemical Theory of Olfaction. 2. Elucidation of the Stereochemical Properties of the Olfactory Receptor Sites', *Proc. Sci. Sect., Toilet Goods Assn.*, Special Supplement to No. 37, pp. 13–23, 1962.

J. E. AMOORE. 'Stereochemical Theory of Olfaction', *Nature*, **198**, 271–272, 1963.

L. H. BECK and W. R. MILES. 'Some Theoretical and Experimental Relationships Between Infrared Absorption and Olfaction', *Science*, **106**, 511, 1947.

L. H. BECK and W. R. MILES. 'Infrared Absorption in Field Studies of Olfaction in Honey Bees', *Proc. Nat. Acad. Sci.*, **35**, 292–310, 1949.

M. G. J. BEETS. 'Odour and Molecular Constitution', *Am. Perfumer and Aromatics*, **76**, No. 6, 54–63, 1961.

M. GUILLOT. (Some Characteristics of the Phenomenon of Partial Anosmia.) *C. r., Soc. Biol.*, Paris, **142**, 161–162, 1948.

M. GUILLOT. (Physiology of the Senses. Partial Anosmia and Fundamental Odours.) *Compt. rend. Acad. Sci.*, Paris, **226**, 1307–1309, 1948.

J. W. JOHNSTON. 'Infrared Loss Theory of Olfaction Untenable', *Phys. Zool.*, **26**, No. 3, 266–273, 1953.

J. W. JOHNSTON and A. B. PARKS. 'Odour Intensity and the Stereochemical Theory of Olfaction', *Proc. Sci. Sect., Toilet Goods Assn.*, No. 34, 4–7, 1960.

J. W. JOHNSTON and A. SANDOVAL. 'Organoleptic Quality and the Stereochemical Theory of Olfaction', *Proc. Sci. Sect., Toilet Goods Assn.*, **33**, 3–9, 1960.

J. W. JOHNSTON and A. SANDOVAL. 'The Stereochemical Theory of Olfaction. 4. The Validity of Muskiness as a Primary Odour', *Proc. Sci. Sect., Toilet Goods Assn.*, Special Supplement to No. 37, pp. 34–45, 1962.

F. N. JONES and M. H. JONES. 'Modern Theories of Olfaction: A Critical Review', *J. Psychol.*, **36**, 207–241, 1953.

J. LEMAGNEN. (Analysis of Complex and Homologous Odours by Fatigue.) *Compt. rend., Acad. Sci.*, Paris, **226**, 753–754, 1948.

R. W. MONCRIEFF. *The Chemical Senses*. John Wiley, New York. 2nd Edition, 1951.

L. J. MULLINS. 'Olfaction', *Ann. New York Acad. Sci.*, **62**, 249–276, 1955.

D. OTTOSON. 'Some Aspects of the Function of the Olfactory System', *Pharmacological Reviews*, **15**, 1–42, 1963.

M. RUBIN, D. APOTHEKER, and R. LUTMER. 'The Stereochemical Theory of Olfaction. 3. Structure and Odour: 1,4-cyclohexane Lactones and Related Compounds', *Proc. Sci. Sect., Toilet Goods Assn.*, Special Supplement to No. 37, pp. 24–33, 1962.

L. T. TROLAND. *The Principles of Psychophysiology*. Vol. 2. Van Nostrand, New York, 1930.

M. WINTER. (Odour and Constitution. XIX. Homologues and Analogues of 1-*p*-hydroxyphenyl-3-butanone, ketone of the raspberry.) *Helv. Chim. Acta*, **44**, No. 7, 2110–2121, 1961.

17

Enter the Quantum

'OUR mental picture, therefore, of a molecule of an odourous substance, such, for example, as benzaldehyde, may be taken as that of
an assemblage of atoms arranged in the accepted configuration of
the organic chemist—but these atoms are not static; they move
about a mean position and are dynamic in the sense that they have a
periodic motion with regard to their fellow atoms. Not all such
motions are perceptible to the osmic sensory system, but certain of
them which are so perceptible constitute the *osmic frequencies* of the
molecule, and it is these which are able to affect the sensitive membranes of the nose and so give rise to the sensation of smell.'
This very clear statement of the vibrational hypothesis of odour
was given in a paper published by G. M. Dyson in 1937. Dyson came
to this general conclusion as a result of his work with the mustard
oils some years earlier—at a time when the fact that molecules could
vibrate was understood, but before there were any experimental
techniques for recording or measuring the vibrations. By 1937 the
situation had changed, and, for the first time, there was a well-
understood way to chart the internal, vibratory movements of
molecules—and this has since been reinforced by a second method.
These two investigational tools are known respectively as the Raman
Effect and Infrared Spectroscopy.
To understand in a general way how they work, we must go back
to first principles.
An electric charge, or an electrically charged object, will attract
or repel other charges or charged objects with a force that depends
on the sizes of the charges and the distance between them. As long
as the values of the charges are fixed and their positions are fixed,
the force between them is fixed; but if one of the charges moves the
force changes, and if the charge moves from side to side across the
line joining the charges, the force on the other body fluctuates.
(Movement back and forth along the line that joins the charges need
not be considered here.) The fluctuations in the force on the second
charge do not coincide exactly with the movements of the first one
because it takes a certain length of time for the effect to travel
through the space between the two bodies. The electrical disturbance

travels with the speed of light, and, indeed, if the oscillations of the first charge are rapid enough, the disturbance it sends out into space *is* light. The 'waves of light' the physicists speak of are the periodic fluctuations in the electrostatic forces emanating from an oscillating electric charge.

In addition to the electric forces there are magnetic forces, because a moving electric charge is what we call an electric current. Anyone who brings a compass needle near a wire carrying a current can see that the moving charges generate magnetic forces. If the charge moves back and forth, the direction of the magnetic force reverses every time the current reverses, and these changes in the magnetic force are not propagated instantly through space, but rather they spread out with the velocity of light—just like the electric oscillations.

Thus a stationary electric charge is surrounded by a static electric field and no magnetic forces, but an oscillating charge generates fluctuating electric *and* magnetic forces in the space around it, and these oscillations travel out together with the same very high velocity of approximately 3×10^{10} centimetres per second, which is commonly denoted by the letter 'c'. Because both electric and magnetic forces are involved, the disturbance is called 'electromagnetic radiation'. If the oscillation is rather slow (low frequency) the radiation is what we call 'radio frequency'—which can range all the way from the long-wave broadcast bands to the ultra-high-frequencies used in radar and microwave telecommunications. At still higher frequencies we have infrared or heat rays, then visible light, and then ultraviolet and X-radiation.

If the velocity of the radiation through space is c cm. per second, and if the radiating charge moves back and forth with a frequency of ν times per second, then there will be ν waves sent out in one second and they will be spread over a distance of c cm., so that each single wave will extend over a distance, or 'wavelength', λ, of c/ν. Thus the three quantities: wavelength, λ, velocity, c, and frequency, ν, are related by the formula,

$$c = \nu\lambda$$

For various practical reasons, it is easier to measure the wavelength than the frequency, so that the frequency is best arrived at indirectly, by calculation:

$$\nu = \frac{c}{\lambda}$$

However, this involves the velocity of light, c, which is known only approximately, and if the wavelengths are transformed into frequencies with this formula the frequencies have to be re-calculated every time someone re-measures the speed of light. To avoid this, it is customary to calculate $1/\lambda$ instead of c/λ. While c/λ is the true frequency, or number of oscillations per second, $1/\lambda$ is often called the 'frequency' also, although it is really the number of waves per centimetre, and so is more properly known as the 'wave number'. To change from wave number to frequency we need only multiply by the speed of light, c.

It has been known since the beginning of the century that chemical atoms are built up of positive and negative electric charges, so that oscillating movements of molecules and atoms, or parts of them, can produce electromagnetic radiation or interact with it in various ways. These interactions are involved in the Raman Effect and in the absorption of infrared rays.

In absorption measurements, for example, radiation of many wavelengths is sent through a sample of the material being studied, and certain wavelengths whose frequency matches or resonates with the frequency of the molecular vibrations are absorbed. The unabsorbed radiation that passes through the sample is then spread out into a spectrum by means of a prism, and the places are charted where radiation is missing due to the absorption. The frequency of the missing radiation in these 'absorption bands' corresponds directly to the vibrational frequencies of the molecules that produced the absorption. Thus, in principle, it is fairly easy to chart the vibrational frequencies of molecules—but the apparatus with which you do it is complex and expensive. A spectrometer for the 'near infrared' costs anywhere from $5000 to $20,000, and for work in the far infrared (which, as we shall see, is of most interest in relation to smell) there has until recently been no apparatus at all available commerically. You invented and built your own or went without. Since 1961, a few far infrared machines have been produced commercially, but the price of a 1963 model is about $35,000. This is a sordid detail but an important one, and it explains why the modern researcher must at times forsake the pursuit of knowledge for the pursuit of financial help. There are not many fields left where the research can be done in a wood-shed and with apparatus made from sealing wax and string.

Aside from the difficulty and cost of getting the equipment, an infrared absorption spectrum is basically a fairly simple matter. The Raman Effect, which is the alternative way to explore molecular vibrations, is a little more difficult to understand, because it involves the Quantum Theory.

141

In 1900, Max Planck found that when a particle or an electric charge of atomic or molecular dimensions is given an oscillating or to-and-fro motion, the amount of energy of motion it can have is limited to certain discrete quantities, or 'quanta'. It can oscillate with one 'quantum' of energy, or 2, or 3, or any whole number of quanta, but not with any fractional number. The size of the quantum, that is, the unit amount of energy the oscillator can take up, depends on the characteristic frequency, v (which, in turn, depends on the forces and masses involved), and is described by the formula:

$$E = nhv$$

where E is the energy of the oscillator, v is the frequency in oscillations per second, h is a universal constant known as Planck's Constant, and $n = 0$, or 1, or 2, or whatever whole number of quanta the oscillator happens to have.

If you ask, 'Why is this so?' physics can give no answer except to say that it is the way things are.

The Raman Effect as a way of charting molecular vibrations depends on the fact that these vibrations are subject to the quantum rules because they are oscillations in a structure that is of molecular dimensions. If you pass electromagnetic radiation of a single frequency (monochromatic light) through a transparent substance, some of the molecules may absorb energy from the radiation and be set into vibration. If the frequency of the incident radiation is v_i, its energy is given by hv_i. When energy is taken from the radiation by the molecular oscillators, its energy and therefore its frequency is reduced to a new value, v_0, such that:

$$\text{energy abstracted} = hv_i - hv_0$$

But the energy was abstracted by a molecule that was set to vibrating with a frequency, v, of its own, and since the energy lost by the radiation must be equal to that gained by the molecule,

$$hv = hv_i - hv_0$$

or,

$$v = v_i - v_0$$

Thus, if we can measure the *difference* in frequency of the incident light and the light scattered by the molecules after they have abstracted enough energy to be set vibrating, the difference gives the vibrational frequency of the molecule directly.

142

But since the method only works with transparent substances, most of the incident light goes right through the sample unchanged. The depleted quanta that are left after the molecules of the sample have abstracted their vibrational quanta, are scattered off in all directions at extremely low intensities. The scattered radiation can be photographed and analyzed by viewing the sample against a dark background from a direction at right angles to the path of the incoming radiation—but it needs very sensitive equipment to collect and measure the scattered light, and the technique is troublesome and difficult, especially when you have to work with complex and often unstable organic chemicals, which is what so many perfumes seem to be.

Dyson's theory of odour was based on the hypothesis that the physical basis of odour lies not in the size or shape or chemical reactivity of the odourous molecules, but in their vibrational movements. In a general way this is a most attractive idea because it offers such a simple and general explanation of one of the most puzzling things about smells: the fact that things with very different structures may smell alike (the musks, for example), and things with very similar structures may smell differently (such as the ketones shown on page 108). A molecule is essentially a collection of massive particles held together with elastic forces, and the same mechanical, vibrational frequency can be associated with a variety of quite different chemical structures and chemical properties.

In 1937, when Dyson suggested that the then recently discovered Raman Effect would make it possible to put his vibrational hypothesis on an experimental basis, the characteristic and specific vibrational frequencies of only a few molecules had been charted, and the technique was rather specialized. Dyson, himself, was not a spectroscopist (if he had been he would probably not have been interested in odours) and so he had to use whatever data had been published by others in the technical literature. With the information he could collect, he suggested that the 'osmic frequencies' to which the nose is sensitive corresponded to wave numbers between 1400 and 3500, and that, for example, ethereal odours were due to frequencies around 2700 wave numbers, and so on. He also stressed the fact that besides having the appropriate vibrational frequencies, an odourous substance must be sufficiently volatile and have the right solubility characteristics.

Thus the vibrational hypothesis is eminently plausible, and, what is much more unusual, it is basically capable of being verified experimentally and in detail. All that is necessary is to compare the vibrational frequencies of groups of substances with similar odours, and to show that the odour correlates with certain vibrational frequencies or combinations of frequencies.

If this is all that is needed, and if the infrared and Raman techniques are available and applicable, why has this test not been applied? What are we waiting for? As this book is partly the story of how research is actually done as well as an account of what comes out of it, I must answer the question by recounting a story of fumblings and mistakes and partly-correct ideas, not very different from the ones I described in Chapter 3.

When Dyson's theory was put forward it attracted a good deal of interest, but it was soon shelved because his particular odour-frequency correlations in the 1400 to 3500 wave number range would not stand up. They did not predict odours from frequencies correctly, and so failed to meet the most important requirement of a good theory.

What was overlooked for nearly twenty years was the fact that the basic idea could be right and the particular assignment of osmic frequencies could be wrong, and so the baby was thrown out along with the bath water. It is easy to see this now, after the event, but the fact is that along with everyone else, I was able to work on the problem at intervals for several years without realizing that the question had never been properly put.

A moment ago I said that molecular vibrations are quantized, and that a molecular vibration must have at least one quantum of energy or else remain inactive. In general, there are only a few sources from which a molecule can draw this energy. In a flame it can come from the chemical energy of a reaction—but there are no flames in the nose. Outside of a flame but within sight of it, the molecule can receive its energy by radiation—but it is dark inside the nose, so that radiative excitation of the vibrations of the odourous molecules is also ruled out. This leaves only one source of energy to excite the vibrations of the molecule, and that is the collisions it makes with the nitrogen and oxygen molecules of the air.

Now the violence of these inter-molecular collisions is directly related to the absolute temperature, and under conditions as they exist in the nose, this is not far from 30° to 35°C, or, say, an absolute temperature of about 300°K. This is a relatively low temperature so that there is not a great amount of energy available to activate the vibrational movements, and therefore only the low-energy vibrations can be set going by collision. The size of a quantum of vibrational energy is given by $h\nu$, and so a small energy means a small value of ν (that is, a low frequency), and *vice versa*. In 1953, I calculated the average number of quanta of vibrational energy that could be given to vibrators of various frequencies by collisions with air molecules at 300°K, with the following results:

Wave number frequency	Average number of vibrational quanta per molecule
1000	0·008
800	0·022
600	0·059
400	0·17
200	0·62
100	1·62
50	3·69

This shows that with molecules having a vibrational frequency corresponding to 1000 wave numbers, only one molecule in every 125 will be vibrating and the remaining 124 will be 'silent' (because 1/125 = 0·008). At 400 wave numbers, the proportion of vibrationally active molecules is 1 in 6, and not until the frequency is well under 200 wave numbers does each molecule have on the average one quantum of vibrational energy.

Evidently, then, only the frequencies below about 500 wave numbers are appreciably activated by collisions with air molecules at 300°K, and Dysons' 'osmic frequencies' between 1400 and 3500 wave numbers cannot possibly be right. The proper place to look for osmic frequencies is in the region between, say, 500 and 50 wave numbers.

It is exceedingly unfortunate from the standpoint of odour theory that vibrations in this frequency range have gone largely unstudied, for a combination of reasons.

For one thing, the spectrum of scattered light that we photograph includes both the very faint Raman lines and a much stronger line due to part of the light from the source being scattered with unaltered frequency. The low frequency Raman lines lie very close to this strong line and are hard to see, and for that reason the information is usually incomplete at the low end of the frequency range. Similarly, in the infrared spectrum, frequencies between 500 and 50 wave numbers correspond to rather long wavelengths (between 20 and 200 microns), and until very recently there were probably fewer than half a dozen machines in the whole world capable of adequately exploring this part of the infrared spectrum. Their owners usually used them to study simpler molecules than the general run of perfume chemicals.

To these experimental and instrumental difficulties, one must add the fact that these frequencies have not been very interesting theoretically to chemists and physicists, most of whom have not been concerned with smells, or aware that they might possibly depend on molecular vibrations.

Probably this is the reason also why some of the criticisms of the vibrational theory have been so wide of the mark. Dyson's basic vibrational hypothesis may or may not be correct, but it is wrong to rule it out on the grounds that the higher frequencies do not correlate with odour—as was done by more than one critic. One man, for example, examined the compounds methyl cyanide, $CH_3C{\equiv}N$, and methyl isocyanide, $CH_3{-}N{\equiv}C$, which have quite different odours, and found the following frequencies (the list is not complete and there may be additional, undiscovered lines, especially at the low end of the range):

Methyl cyanide	Methyl isocyanide
3009·0	3014·3
2965·3	2965·8
2267·3	2166·0
1454·0	1459·0
1400·0	1410·0
1041·0	1130·0
919·9	944·6
361·0	270·0

From the standpoint of odour theory, only the frequencies below 500 are important and the difference there is most suggestive. The near identity of the higher frequencies is totally irrelevant, and yet this pair of compounds was cited as evidence *against* the theory that odour depends on low frequency vibrations. I mention this only because the writer in question has been rather widely quoted as having 'disproved' the vibrational theory, mainly by people who have looked at his conclusions without examining his reasoning.

Some other critics have supposed that Dyson was suggesting that it was the Raman Effect itself that was somehow creating the olfactory sensations. This is about as wild a misunderstanding as could be imagined, and, so that there can be no possibility of a mistake, let me summarize the theory once more:

1. It is assumed that odour sensations have their origin in certain vibrational movements of the odorous molecules.

2. For quantum reasons, the vibrations in question must have a rather low frequency, and probably lie in the range 500 to 50 wave numbers.

3. The only available techniques for measuring the vibrational movements of molecules experimentally are based on the Raman Effect and Infrared Spectroscopy.

4. If the appropriate vibrational frequencies of various odourous substances are measured, it should be possible (if the theory is correct) to correlate the odours with the possession of certain frequencies or combinations of frequencies.

5. The nature of the interaction between the vibrating, odourous molecules and the olfactory cells of the nose is unknown, but there is no reason to suppose that it depends on either the Raman scattering or the infrared absorption phenomena that are used in the laboratory to chart the frequencies.

In the next chapter I will look at this theory in rather more detail, but I must warn you that I like this theory and my account of it will not be impartial.

REFERENCES

G. M. DYSON. 'The Raman Effect and the Concept of Odour', *Perfum. and Essen. Oil Record*, **28**, 13–19, 1937.

G. M. DYSON. 'The Scientific Basis of Odour', *Chem. and Ind.*, London, **16**, 647–651, 1938.

H. W. THOMPSON and R. L. WILLIAMS. 'The Infrared Spectra of Methyl Cyanide and Methyl Isocyanide', *Trans. Faraday Soc.*, **48**, 502–513, 1952.

H. W. THOMPSON. 'Some Comments on Theories of Smell', in 'Molecular Structure and Organoleptic Quality'. S.C.I. Monograph No. 1, Society of Chemical Industry, London, 1957. pp. 103–115.

R. H. WRIGHT. 'Odour and Chemical Constitution', *Nature*, **173**, 831, 1954.

R. H. WRIGHT. 'Odour and Molecular Vibration. I. Quantum and Thermodynamic Considerations', *J. Appl. Chem.*, **4**, 611–615, 1954.

18

A General Theory

IF Dyson's basic conception of 'osmic frequencies' is correct, and if my calculation of their probable range of values is valid, then the molecules of substances with similar odours should be found to have similar low frequency vibrations.

Nitrobenzene, benzonitrile, and alpha-nitro thiophene, all have somewhat almond-like odours and their low frequency vibrations (as far as they have been determined) are shown in the following table. The table also shows the frequencies of benzaldehyde, a compound that is commonly said to be very similar to nitrobenzene but which we found to be only moderately so in a careful experiment with fifteen observers. The low frequencies of butyronitrile are also given because they are quite like those of nitrobenzene and because the first six people I asked to smell a carefully purified sample of it thought that it, too, had something of the almond odour.

Nitrobenzene	Benzonitrile	Nitrothiophene	Butyronitrile	Benzaldehyde
176	172	169	179	130
252				225
	320			237
397	381	376	370	
435	405	442		439
532	460		524	
	549			

I think this shows some indication of a correlation of the almond odour of these compounds with their low frequency vibrations, but it is by no means convincing. One ought to do the same thing with at least a dozen different odours and for frequencies down to 50 wave numbers. (It is quite possible for the substances in the table to have frequencies lower than those shown.)

The number of fundamental frequencies for any molecule can be calculated. For a molecule made up of n atoms, the number of independent vibrational movements it can execute (usually called its 'normal modes') is $(3n - 6)$, or, for the special case where the atoms all lie on a straight line, $(3n - 5)$. Thus, for a simple molecule with two atoms (like O_2, which can be pictured as O=O), $3n - 5 = 1$, and the two atoms can move in and out as though joined by a spring.

Carbon dioxide is a straight-line molecule with three atoms: $O{=}C{=}O$, and $3n - 5 = 4$. These four modes can be pictured as follows:

1. The C fixed and the two O's moving in and out together.
2. The two O's fixed and the C moving to and fro between them.
3. The two O's fixed and the C moving in and out of the paper.
4. The two O's fixed and the C moving up and down in the paper.

(Modes 3 and 4 would have exactly the same frequency, and are said to be 'degenerate', but they are basically distinct because each could happen without the other.)

Water, H_2O, has a V-shaped molecule: H⟍ ⟋H over O , in which $n = 3$,

so that $(3n - 6) = 3$, which can be described approximately as:

1. The two H's moving in and out from the O together.
2. One H moving in as the other moves out.
3. The bonds bending so that the two H's wave to and fro.

With more complicated molecules, the movements become more complicated and harder to describe either with words or pictures, but the number of possible 'normal modes' is always precisely calculable from the formulae $(3n - 6)$ or $(3n - 5)$ and theorists are beginning to be able to make 'assignments' of the observed frequencies to the various modes, at least for the fairly simple molecules.

It turns out that not all the lines observed in a Raman or infrared spectrum represent fundamental or normal modes. There can be overtones, and two different fundamentals can co-operate to produce a 'combination band'. This is why there are often more lines than modes. The frequencies of the combination lines are approximately (but not exactly) the sums of the normal modes that produce them, which usually makes them big enough to fall outside the range of our osmic frequencies, 50 to about 500 wave numbers. A more serious difficulty arises with certain rather symmetrical molecules which have normal modes that for certain reasons do not produce infrared absorption or Raman scattering. The lowest observed infrared band of pyridine, for example, is at 405 wave numbers, but there is a lower frequency at 374 wave numbers which appears in the Raman spectrum. When the detailed assignments are made, this 374 frequency turns out to be the lowest. Ordinary pyridine, by the way, has a powerful and most unpleasant smell, but when it is rigorously purified it has little or no smell and is not unpleasant.

From the standpoint of odour theory, one should try to correlate the smell with the frequencies of the normal modes, and if they are not known because the detailed assignments have not been made, then one must take the observed infrared and Raman frequencies as the next best thing.

This is an important point because it draws attention to the fact that it is the molecular vibrations themselves that we assume to be triggering the smell sensations, and *not* the Raman scattering or the infrared absorption derived from them. This point has been so constantly misunderstood by critics of the theory, that I must illustrate it by one more example. The vibration of a drum can be perceived by the noise it makes, or it can be felt with the fingers, or it can be made visible by putting a few dried peas on the drum head. These are three distinct techniques for registering the vibration of the drum, using, respectively, our ears, our fingers, and our eyes. The Raman Effect, infrared spectroscopy, *and the nose*, are three distinct techniques for registering the vibrations of molecules.

The ability to calculate the total number of 'normal modes' of vibration poses a somewhat embarrassing question to the vibrational theory right at the outset. There are a few substances with simple molecules which have well-known smells and *no* low frequency vibrations. The most important of them are:

H_2S	HCN	NH_3
1290	712	932
2611	2089	968
2684	3312	1628
		3336
		3338
		3414

These look like serious obstacles to the theory but they are not insurmountable.

In the presence of water, hydrogen sulphide can be oxidized (usually rather slowly) to form H_2O and S, but several intermediate oxidation products are known which could be formed by such reactions as:

$$4H_2S + O_2 = 2H_2O + 2H_2S_2$$
$$2H_2S_2 = H_2S + H_2S_3$$

Hydrogen persulphide, H_2S_2, is chemically analogous to hydrogen peroxide, and the other polysulphides (or 'sulphanes') do have low frequency Raman lines:

H_2S_2	H_2S_3	H_2S_4
509	210	185
883	483	229
2509	862	450
	2502	483
		862
		2501

So far, I have not been able to think of a way to prove that H_2S_2 or H_2S_3 is really formed in our noses when we inhale a mixture of H_2S and air, but I can cite two pieces of evidence which suggest that it very well may be. The first is the fact that Baradi and Bourne found a considerable variety of enzymes in the olfactory mucous membranes, not necessarily in the olfactory cells themselves, but in various closely associated tissues. These probably include some oxidizing enzymes (oxidases). There is also the fact that H_2S is a very poisonous gas—as toxic as hydrogen cyanide, HCN, but not as dangerous because its smell usually gives plenty of warning. To be so toxic, it must react, and react quickly, with the tissues it touches. Thus the H_2S obstacle is not insuperable.

As for HCN, it also is a reactive gas, and toxic, and the fact that some people cannot smell it points to the possibility that they lack the special chemical point of attachment it needs to generate an osmic frequency.

The 'smell' of ammonia when strong is mainly or wholly a pain sensation, and at high dilutions this may still be the main component, possibly combined with a response to the alkaline reaction this very soluble gas has when in solution.

Apart from the difficulty presented by these three compounds, the vibration theory accounts smoothly for all the varied phenomena I have described in the earlier chapters.

For example, the general similarity or identity of the smells of the optically isomeric compounds described in Chapter 15 is exactly what the vibrational theory would predict. The frequencies of the normal modes of the left- and right-handed forms of a compound are exactly the same, and therefore their odours should be exactly the same, unless the molecular asymmetry allows one form to link itself a little more closely to the asymmetric molecules of the olfactory cells. In certain cases this could engender a slightly different smell intensity or 'note', but the difference between the two members of an optically isomeric pair should never be very great—and in fact it never is.

As for the informational capacity of the olfactory system (discussed in Chapter 11), the vibrational theory is the first, and indeed the only theory of the olfactory process to meet its demands adequately. The frequency range 50 to 500 wave numbers comprises something over three 'octaves'. On the piano this corresponds to 35–40 distinct tones, and if the 'bandwidths' of the separate osmic frequencies are about the same as those of the notes on a piano, the twenty-five to thirty-five primary odours which information theory requires (see page 84) are nicely accounted for.

151

Again, the phenomena of partial anosmia and selective fatigue studied by Guillot, LeMagnen and others (see Chapter 16) fit in very well. You can do a very simple experiment with red and white clover blossoms to see what this is all about. Both blossoms have a rather similar 'floral' odour, but if you smell a white blossom for a few moments and immediately thereafter sniff at a red one, you will find that you cannot perceive the scent of the red one for several seconds. Smelling the white blossom has fatigued your nose so that it cannot immediately smell the red one. If you now reverse the order, and smell the red clover first, you will find that it does *not* prevent you from smelling the white one immediately.

The vibrational theory explains this and various similar cases very simply. If + represents the presence of a particular osmic frequency, and if − denotes the absence of a frequency, then the white and red clover patterns might be represented like this:

```
white:  − + − − − + − + − − + + − − − − − + − + + −
red:    − + − − − − − + − − + − − − − − − − − + − −
```

Evidently smelling the white clover first would fatigue all the receptor organs for the red, but if the red was smelled first one would still perceive enough of the white frequencies to recognize the pattern.

We do something very like this with our ears. A violinist plays a chord, such as C minor, by bowing no more than two strings simultaneously. An organist can play as many as ten notes simultaneously by using both hands. The C-minor chord of the organist is recognizably similar to that of the violinist, but richer in fundamental frequencies. If our ears were as readily fatigued as our noses, the organist could make us temporarily deaf to a C minor chord played by a violinist, but the violinist could not prevent us from hearing the organist's C minor chord.

If the receptors for certain osmic frequencies are congenitally absent instead of being temporarily fatigued, you will have cases of partial anosmia of exactly the kind reported by Guillot (Chapter 16) or Blakeslee (Chapter 13).

The theory also explains many things I have not taken up in any detail in the preceding chapters. The subtle (and sometimes not so subtle) effects of impurities on the odours of substances are very important to perfumers, gourmets, and connoisseurs of fine wines. One can easily see how a blending of two odours each of which has an osmic frequency at a sub-threshold level could produce an unexpectedly rich result. In other cases, the removal of a certain frequency contributed by an impurity could 'refine' an odour in a highly desirable way.

152

If the vibrational theory can be put on a secure foundation by an ironclad correlation of low frequency modes with particular odours or the ability to attract particular insects or fishes, there will be an immense field for research into all these matters.

In the meantime, there is one thing more to consider here: the possible way the vibrating, odourous molecules interact with the olfactory cells so as to generate signals in the axons leading to the olfactory bulb. I began this book with a story of research as it actually gets done, and I might finish it with another.

When I first began to think and talk about molecular vibrations as a cause of odour, I was regularly asked by other chemists how a molecular oscillation—and especially a low frequency, low energy one—could possibly trigger a nerve impulse. When I passed the question on to men who were experts in matters of nerve physiology, the answer I got was, in effect: 'We are sorry we can't help you, but the truth is that when you come right down to it, we don't really know how *any* nerve signals are actually initiated'.

This was more helpful than it sounds, because it left the field wide open to informed speculation. To help me with this I was lucky in my friends, among whom Dr. C. Reid was especially willing to think imaginatively and constructively about the problem.

As it turned out, my part was to supply the olfactory facts while he contributed a wide knowledge of the chemistry and chemical energetics of various living processes. After many hours of discussion (often over lunch, and with a heavy consumption of scribbled-over paper place mats) we evolved a theory of the triggering process that looked fairly reasonable. The next thing was to write it down in detail and to ask half-a-dozen scientists of various sorts to look at it and make suggestions. Most of them said, politely, that it was an interesting theory, but one of them, the late Dr. H. G. V. Evans, took it to heart and spent several days and nights in detailed calculations which showed that the theory as it stood could not account for the very low thresholds that many odours exhibit (see Chapter 7). By developing our basic idea in a somewhat different way, he overcame the difficulty. All this was spread over five or six months and a great deal of paper was torn up by night as well as by day before we were done.

The result was a theory of olfactory stimulation that may be true or may not, but which is consistent with as much basic chemistry and physics, physiology and anatomy, and general olfactory background as we could make it.

The primary clue we started from is the fact that the olfactory mucous membranes of the nose are coloured a distinctive yellow or brown by a substance known as the 'olfactory pigment'. The composition and constitution of this substance are unknown, but it is reported to be present in largest amount in the tissues of animals with the most highly developed noses. We felt that the presence of a coloured substance in the olfactory cells was significant, not because the perception of smell has anything to do with the perception of colour, but because coloured compounds owe their colour to certain peculiarities of their structure that might be relevant to our problem in another way.

A chemical is visibly coloured when its molecules can preferentially absorb light of certain wavelengths. (White light is light of all wavelengths, and if you subtract some of them, what is left is necessarily coloured.) The power to absorb light depends on there being electrons in the structure which can absorb energy from some source and so become raised to an 'excited' level. Thus the colouration of the olfactory tissue is evidence that it contains a substance with easily excitable electrons. Since it is usually dark inside the nose, the pigment molecules would not normally be excited by absorbing light, but they could just as well become excited by absorbing energy from the chemical reactions that are always going on in the living cells around them.

Usually when molecules become electronically excited, the electrons fall back to the 'ground state' rather quickly. Sometimes, however, they are only able to do so after a considerable delay because the return is 'forbidden'. (The phenomenon of phosphorescence is an example of this: light is stored up in a compound and released rather slowly, causing it to glow in the dark for some time after the light is turned off.) The physical theory of these electron transitions is fairly well understood, and the return of the electron is known to be governed (or described) by a mathematical expression called the 'transition moment integral' which looks like this:

$$\int_{-\infty}^{+\infty} \psi_U{}^\star M \psi_L d\tau$$

If this function is zero or very small, the de-excitation of the electron is forbidden, and if the function is large the de-excitation will happen instantaneously. What the integral gives is the probability that the transition will take place.

There are at least two ways that the expression could be zero. The first requires that the part of the integral from $-\infty$ to 0 should be exactly equal and opposite to the part from 0 to $+\infty$. This would require that the pigment molecule be highly symmetrical, and was our first assumption and the one Dr. Evans rejected. In its place, he

154

pointed out that the integral could also be zero if the quantity $\psi_U{}^\star$ was always 0 when ψ_L was not, and *vice versa*. The symbols $\psi_U{}^\star$ and ψ_L represent the vibrations (more strictly, the vibrational wave functions) of the pigment molecule in its upper, or excited, state and in its lower or ground state respectively. The technical way of saying that one is always zero when the other is not is to say that there is no 'overlap' between them.

It is not easy to give this a simple physical interpretation, except to say that there would be no overlap between two wave systems if they were permanently out of phase: if one was always 'up' when the other was 'down'. This can only happen if the two wave trains have exactly the same frequency.

Our picture of an olfactory pigment molecule is of one that can be raised to an electronically excited state rather easily, and whose vibrational wave functions have exactly the same frequency in the upper as in the lower state. If such a molecule becomes electronically excited it will tend to stay that way. Moreover, its electronic excitation will tend to make it electrically polar. If it is situated in the membrane of an olfactory cell, its electrical polarity will probably be aligned with the electrical polarity we know to exist in the membranes of nerve cells, and if something happens to make the electron in the pigment return to the ground state, this would mean a localized depolarization which, as we saw in Chapter 12, is probably the beginning of a nerve impulse.

The next thing was to ask how the nearby presence of an odourous molecule could change the amount of 'overlap' between the upper and lower wave functions, and so allow the electron to return to the ground state.

It is a well-known fact that when two vibrating systems are coupled together they interact more or less strongly, or resonate, when they have the same or nearly the same frequency. A quantitative study of resonance shows that the resonant frequency is not exactly the same as that of the two vibrators when they are by themselves and not coupled together. Depending on the strength of the coupling, the resonant frequency is more or less different from the separate frequencies of the two oscillators.

It follows that if a vibrating odourous molecule becomes coupled with a pigment molecule, and if their vibrational frequencies are the same, or nearly the same, they will resonate and the resonant frequency will not be exactly the same as the normal value of $\psi_U{}^\star$ for the pigment molecule, and so there will be some overlap with ψ_L, and the return of the electron will be allowed.

Our picture of the primary smell detector of an insect or other

155

creature sensitive to a single osmic frequency is therefore rather simple: bare nerve cell walls which contain 'pigment' molecules whose electronic excitation can be discharged by contact with a molecule having the right vibrational frequency, matching that of the pigment. This, incidentally, accounts nicely for the existence of chemicals that can act as sex-attractants for particular insects even though they are quite unrelated chemically to the real sex-attractant.

An animal with a more highly developed nose, that is, one with more informational capacity, will have basically the same equipment, but variegated by the presence of several kinds of olfactory cells, each sensitive to a different frequency. For this to be possible, the structure of the olfactory pigment would have to be modified slightly from one cell type to the next so as to have a different frequency in each type. In a creature with twenty-five types of end organ and sensitive to twenty-five 'primary' odours, this would mean twenty-five variants on the basic pigment molecule. This is by no means inconceivable, and in fact the observed brown colour of the olfactory tissues is more consistent with a multiplicity of optical absorbers than a single type, which would be more likely to give a red, yellow, green or blue colour than a brown one.

Cases of partial anosmia would be due simply to a congenital inability of the body to make certain variants of the pigment molecule.

The very low threshold concentrations of many odourous substances fit well into the theory, especially when taken in conjunction with the ideas of Davies and Taylor, described in Chapter 13. They calculate the olfactory threshold taking into account the tendency of the molecules to collect in the region of the cell surface, and their ability to 'puncture' the cell membrane. They assumed that the puncturing power was directly proportional to the cross-sectional area of the molecule. On our theory, the threshold would be calculated in almost exactly the same way, except that we would use the bonding force between the odourous molecule and the pigment where they used the cross-sectional area. This force would probably be at least partly related to the size of the odourous molecules, so that the numerical agreement between Davies' and Taylor's calculated and observed thresholds is not surprising.

Another thing that our theory explains is the fact that we can only perceive a smell while the air is moving through our noses. The sensation stops when the sniffing stops. If we picture an odorous molecule attaching itself to a pigment molecule and triggering an electronic de-excitation, the 'jumping down' of the electron would be a rather energetic event from a molecular point of view. It is likely

156

that this would expel the odourous molecule from the surface rather violently. If the air was not moving, the molecule could only find its way back to the surface by slow and random diffusion, but if the air was moving it would be likely to impinge on the sensitive surface again and again.

This theory has been looked at by several qualified specialists who make the perfectly correct remark that it is quite possible in a technical sense, but that there is not a shred of direct evidence that it is really true. (One critic condemned it without understanding it: he supposed that we were claiming that the coupling of the odourous and pigment molecules somehow changed the *energy* of the electronic transition. What we claimed was something completely different: a change in its *probability*.)

I suppose that the most direct test of the theory would be to isolate the olfactory pigment from some animal and to show that it was a mixture of several pigments, each with a distinct low frequency mode (or modes), and that these modes had the same frequencies as the odourous substances the animal was known to respond to. I expect that this test will be applied eventually, but it will take anything up to five years of work and might cost as much as a tenth of one jet fighter aircraft.

Meanwhile, the theory has had one or two interesting aftermaths. It occurred to us to wonder what kind of molecule would be likely to have the properties we attributed to the olfactory pigment, and on reflection it appeared that a chemical something like vitamin A would meet most of the requirements. We mentioned this in our paper along with a report by LeMagnen and Rapaport that rats deprived of vitamin A appeared to lose their sense of smell.

In Australia, Dr. M. H. Briggs and Dr. R. B. Duncan picked up this idea and analysed the tissues of dogs and cows and found strong indications of vitamin A (or something like it) in the olfactory cells. They then found fifty-six people with uncomplicated anosmia (inability to smell even though the olfactory apparatus appeared to be intact), and they gave them large doses of vitamin A intramuscularly. Fifty of the fifty-six patients recovered their power of olfaction in part or completely.

Shortly afterwards, another scientist using another and possibly less specific method of analysis, examined the olfactory tissues of a cow, sixty-one rats, and three pigs. He found evidence of vitamin A in the cow but not in the tissues from the rats or pigs. He therefore argued that the olfactory pigment was not related to vitamin A, which was a fair inference from his experiments. But then he went on to argue that this showed that the olfactory pigment has nothing

157

to do with olfaction—and that therefore the whole vibrational theory must be wrong!

It may very well *be* wrong, but a failure to find vitamin A in the olfactory cells does not prove it.

These two incidents illustrate the usefulness of a good theory in provoking experiments which might not otherwise be conceived. They show that the whole subject of smells and smelling is in a very healthy condition because there are more questions than answers, and more ways of looking for the answers than ever before. The next years should see new advances and interesting discoveries that will prove some of the "facts" and many of the ideas in this book to be wrong.

REFERENCES

A. F. BARADI and G. H. BOURNE. 'Localization of Gustatory and Olfactory Enzymes in the Rabbit and the Problems of Taste and Smell', *Nature*, **168**, 977–979, 1951.

M. H. BRIGGS and R. B. DUNCAN. 'Odour Receptors', *Nature*, **191**, 1310–1311, 1961.

M. H. BRIGGS and R. B. DUNCAN. 'Pigment and the Olfactory Mechanism', *Nature*, **195**, 1313–1314, 1962.

K. BUIJS, C. J. H. SCHUTTE, and F. VERSTER. 'Absence of Correlation Between Odour and Molecular Vibration', *Nature*, **192**, 751–752, 1961.

A. DADIEU. (Studies in the Raman Effect. XI. Raman Spectra of Organic Substances (Cyanogen Compounds).) *Monatsch.*, **57**, 437–468, 1931.

F. FEHÉR, W. LANE, and G. WINKHAUS. (The Chemistry of Sulfur. XXX. Preparation of Sulphanes: H_2S_2, H_2S_3, H_2S_4, and H_2S_5.) *Z. anorg. u. allgem.*, **288**, 113–122, 1956.

M. A. GEREBTZOFF and E. PHILIPPOT. (Lipids and Olfactory Pigment.) *Acta Oto-Rhino-Laryngolica Belgica*, **11**, 297–300, 1957.

J. H. S. GREEN, W. KYNASTON, and A. S. LINDSEY. 'Vibrational Spectra of Benzene Derivatives. I. Nitrobenzene . . .', *Spectrochim. Acta*, **17**, 486–502, 1961.

J. H. S. GREEN. 'Vibrational Spectra of Benzene Derivatives. II. Assignment and Calculated Thermodynamic Functions for Benzonitrile', *Spectrochim. Acta*, **17**, 607–613, 1961.

J. H. S. GREEN, W. KYNASTON, and H. A. GEBBIE. 'Far Infrared Spectroscopy of Benzene Derivatives by Interferometry', *Nature*, **195**, 595–596, 1962.

J. H. S. GREEN, W. KYNASTON, and H. M. PAISLEY. 'Vibrational Spectra of Monosubstituted Pyridines', *Spectrochim. Acta*, **19**, 549–564, 1963.

G. HERZBERG. *Molecular Spectra and Molecular Structure. II. Infrared and Raman Spectra of Polyatomic Molecules.* Van Nostrand, New York, 1945.

C. HEUSGHEM and M. A. GEREBTZOFF. (Concordant Results of Biochemical and Histochemical Examination of Lipids of the Olfactory Mucosa.) *Compt. rend. Soc. Biol.*, **147**, 540–541, 1953.

J. LEMAGNEN and A. RAPAPORT. (The Role of Vitamin A in the Mechanism of Olfaction in the White Rat.) *Compt. rend. Soc. Biol.*, **145**, 800–803, 1951.

J. MEYER. (The Odour of Hydrocyanic Acid.) *Gasmaske*, **7**, 112, 1935.

D. G. MOULTON. 'Pigment and the Olfactory Mechanism', *Nature*, **195**, 1312–1313, 1962.

K. ONAGAWA. (On the Relationship Between the Grade of Colour at the Olfactory Mucous Membrane and the Sensibility of Olfactory Stimulation.) *J. Physiol. Soc. Japan*, **19**, 189–193, 1957.

E. PHILLIPOT and M. A. GEREBTZOFF. (First Results of the Analysis of the Olfactive Pigment.) *J. Physiol.* (Paris), **50**, 451–452, 1958.

H. W. THOMPSON. 'Some Comments on Theories of Smell', in 'Molecular Structure and Organoleptic Quality'. S.C.I. Monograph No. 1, Society of Chemical Industry, London, 1957. pp. 103–115.

R. H. WRIGHT and R. S. E. SERENIUS. 'Odour and Molecular Vibration. II. Raman Spectra of Substances with the Nitrobenzene Odour', *J. Appl. Chem.*, **4**, 615–621, 1954.

R. H. WRIGHT, C. REID, and H. G. V. EVANS. 'Odour and Molecular Vibration. III. A New Theory of Olfactory Stimulation', *Chemistry and Industry*, 1956, No. 37, 973–977.

R. H. WRIGHT. 'Odour and Molecular Vibration', in 'Molecular Structure and Organoleptic Quality'. S.C.I. Monograph No. 1, Society of Chemical Industry, London, 1957. pp. 91–102.

R. H. WRIGHT. 'Odour and Molecular Vibration', *Nature*, **190**, 1101–1102, 1961.

R. H. WRIGHT. 'Molecular Vibration and Insect Sex Attractants', *Nature*, **198**, 455–459, 1963.

INDEX

161

Date Due

NOV - 4 2005